THE DRAMA

of

REDEMPTION

David Shirley and Joel Wingo

All proceeds from the sale
of this book are given to

MURRIETA MISSION FELLOWSHIP

THE DRAMA OF REDEMPTION
Copyright © 2011 by David Shirley and Joel Wingo

ISBN 978-1-257-90785-4

Published 2011 by Murrieta Mission Fellowship
Murrieta, California

Fifth printing. This book is also available as a downloadable PDF at:
http://www.lulu.com/product/paperback/the-drama-of-
redemption/5952358

The views expressed in works published by Murrieta Mission Fellowship
are those of the author(s) and do not necessarily represent the official
position of Murrieta Mission Fellowship or of Calvary Chapel Bible College.

Scripture quotations, unless otherwise noted, are from the *King James
Version*.

Shirley, David, 1952—
The drama of redemption / David Shirley and Joel Wingo.

1. RELIGION. 2. Bible. 3. Interpretation. I. Shirley, David II. Wingo, Joel

220.6

For the students at Calvary Chapel Bible College

CONTENTS

ACKNOWLEDGMENTS

We wish to acknowledge and thank the pastors and teachers who influenced and contributed to many of the insights found in this book. Although annotation has been kept to a minimum to save space and make the book more readable, a bibliography of the works used in the making of this book is included on page 133. We do not wish to give the impression that all of the material written here is our own original work.

Many thanks to Mattie Alnutt Tatton and Brandy Valdivia Memarian for their miraculous interpretation of left-handed calligraphy! This book would never have been completed without the support and editing of such wonderful sisters in Christ. Thank you. "I give thanks to the LORD for He is good" (Ps. 118:1). James Lee also deserves thanks for his help proofreading the manuscript.

While we alone bear the responsibility for any errors found in this book, all the glory for any valuable perspectives found here belongs to the Lord Jesus Christ, "in whom are hidden all the treasures of wisdom and knowledge" (Col. 2:3).

INTRODUCTION

"And beginning at Moses and all the Prophets, He expounded to them in all the Scriptures the things concerning Himself." –Luke 24:27

Jesus Christ is the key to understanding the unity of the Bible. From the earliest chapters of Genesis to the end of Revelation, from the beginning of world history to its consummation, the Bible reveals God through His works and words in the past, present and future. Although not every biblical author knew Jesus by name, they all were conscious of their need for Him as the Redeemer whom God would provide. Before creating the world, God knew both the need for and the means of the redemption He would provide through Jesus Christ. In every age, God, in His loving-kindness, promised this redemption to humanity in the midst of all our failures, from the Fall onward. The Bible, in each of its eight sections and sixty-six books, is unified in its focus on Jesus Christ, the ultimate revelation of God and the fulfillment of God's history of redemption. He is the fulfillment of every promise of God and the satisfaction of every longing of the human soul.

Our main objective in this book is to discover the unity of the Bible as it presents God's plan of redemption for mankind. This will be a fast-moving special survey from Genesis to Revelation emphasizing the relationship between the major sections of Scripture. The sections of Scripture are unified by the theme of redemption, through which we can discover God's "blueprint" for human history. As we observe how God has worked in this world to provide salvation, our appreciation for God and His Word will grow.

We will approach this study from two points of view: (1) what God has done and is accomplishing in history and (2) what God has spoken or revealed in Scripture.[1]

We hope that as we survey the major sections and books of the Bible, every reader will understand and reflect on God's grace in the History of redemption, and will be filled and illuminated by the Father's wisdom, the Son's humility, and the Spirit's power.

---

[1] For a comparison of traditional views of the unity of the Bible, see Appendix C, p. 127.

FOUNDATIONAL CONCEPTS

The Meaning of Redemption

Redemption, as presented in the Bible, means *deliverance at cost.* It involves paying a price to regain something that would otherwise be forfeited. Redemption is one of the richest images of salvation in the Bible, appearing over 150 times. It pictures the slave markets of the ancient world, where destitute people were doomed to inescapable slavery, unless someone with both the means and the desire to buy them back would pay the price for their liberation.

Most of the biblical references to redemption are found in the Old Testament, where God is pictured as the Redeemer who delivers his people from forced slavery (Ex. 6:6), rescues them from poverty and ruin (the Book of Ruth), forgives and restores them despite their spiritual adultery (Hos. 3), and liberates them from the power of Death itself (Hos. 13:14).

In the New Testament, redemption is used to describe two aspects of salvation:

i)   The completed sacrifice by which Jesus Christ paid the price for salvation on the Cross (Gal. 3:13; Mk. 10:45; 1 Pet. 1:18-19).
ii) The future day when all believers and creation itself will experience full redemption, including the redemption of the human body through the resurrection (Lk. 21:28; Eph. 1:14; Rom. 8:23).

The New Testament references to redemption emphasize the price Jesus paid—his sacrificial death on the Cross—through which we believers have been set free from our slavery to sin.

The biblical image of redemption deserves thoughtful meditation on the part of believers. The history of redemption is not only historical, but also personal. We were helplessly imprisoned as slaves to sin and death, with no way to escape. The cost of our redemption was immeasurably high, yet it has been paid by the death of God's own Son. It is because of this costly sacrifice of God Himself in Jesus Christ that we are forgiven and restored to friendship with God.

In sum, redemption is deliverance from sin's bondage by *a price that is paid* (the Cross) and *power that enables* (the Cross, the Resurrection, Pentecost, and the Return of Christ). It is the process whereby God reinstates human beings to fellowship with Himself. God reveals this slowly, but progressively through the ages, and He has preserved this knowledge in the Bible. All redemptive activity is through Jesus Christ, by the power of God; and it is received by faith.[2]

Three Important Concepts

As we begin to study the History of redemption, the following three concepts will help guide our way:

i)   Redemption is a *work* of God, not merely an *idea*.
ii) Redemption is a *progressive* work of God.
iii) Redemption is a *purposeful* work of God that is moving toward a *goal*.

First, it is important for us to understand that our salvation is based upon an activity, not only upon an idea of God.

> *"But you are not in the flesh but in the Spirit, if indeed the Spirit of God dwells in you. Now if anyone does not have the Spirit of Christ, he is not His. And if Christ is in you, the body is dead because of sin, but the Spirit is life because of righteousness. But if the Spirit of Him who raised Jesus from the dead dwells in you, He who raised Christ from the dead will also give life to your mortal bodies through His Spirit who dwells in you." –Rom. 8:9-11*

> *"And what is the exceeding greatness of His power toward us who believe, according to the working of His mighty power which He worked in Christ when He raised Him from the dead and seated Him at His right hand in the heavenly places, far above all principality and power and might and dominion, and every name that is named, not only in this age but also in that which is to come." –Eph. 1:19-21*

We are not saved by the doctrine of atonement but by the Cross of history. The fundamental unity of the Scriptures is not merely an idea; it is the real, historical work of God. Specifically, it is the work of God concerning the redemption of humankind. Everything else

---

[2] For further reflection on the meaning of Redemption, see Appendix A, p. 115.

in the Bible is related to this main theme of both the Old and New Testaments, the redemption that is in Christ Jesus. Salvation is based on what God has done in the past, is doing in the present, and will do in the future. Throughout Scripture, God is not only working but also speaking: He is explaining His work, exhorting His people to respond to what He is doing, and predicting what He will do in the future. The Bible is the record of the works and words of God. It is His inspired, completed, revelation for transforming the present. Jesus summarized God's method of revelation in Matt. 11:2-4 when He said, "Go tell what you hear and see." Some portions of the Bible, such as the historical books, focus mainly on the works of God while other portions, like the prophetic books, deal primarily with the words of God. However, what God says is always related to what He is doing.

> "Surely the Lord God does nothing, unless He reveals His secret to His servants the prophets. A Lion has roared! Who will not fear? The Lord God has spoken! Who can but prophesy?" – Amos.3:7-8

Second, as we study the History of redemption, we will see that God brings about redemption *progressively*. Every living thing in God's hand grows. In nature, for example, an acorn develops into an oak tree and a tiny cell becomes a fully developed human being. In the same way, after Adam's sin, Cain's murder of Abel, the violence of Noah's day and the pride displayed at the tower of Babel, God's salvation program developed from one man (Abraham) and God's promise to create the great nation through which all the people groups of the earth will find God's blessing. Likewise, the proclamation of the Gospel began with a single witness (Jesus Himself) who passed on the message to a small group of witnesses in a remote corner of the world. Eventually, this group of witnesses grew to proclaim the message of redemption through Christ to the whole world. God's desire to include all nations in His plan of redemption is seen in Psalm 2:8, addressed to His Anointed One:

> "Ask of me, and I shall give thee the heathen for thine inheritance, and the uttermost parts of the earth for thy possession." –Ps. 2:8

Third, God's plan of redemption is moving *purposefully* toward a *goal*. God has a specific goal in mind.

> "But as truly as I [the LORD] live, all the earth shall be filled with the glory of the LORD. –Num. 14:21

"For the earth will be filled with the knowledge of the glory of the Lord, as the waters cover the sea." –Hab. 2:14

God's goal is to fill the earth with His glory. The last two chapters of the Bible, Revelation 21 and 22, describe God filling the new heaven and earth with the light of His unmediated presence, which does away with the need for the light of the sun or moon. Although the history of redemption has not yet reached its destination, God is carrying out His plan. The glory of God has already been revealed in His coming to earth, and God is presently filling the earth with "the knowledge of the glory of the Lord" through people who have been rescued from the bonds of sin and death, who are living like Jesus Christ, and who are proclaiming His salvation to the world through their changed lives and verbal testimony of the Gospel. In light of this, the goal of life for the Christian is the image of God restored.

The three concepts explained above help us understand the unity and diversity of the Scriptures. The Bible has many different components: different human authors with different perspectives, different literary forms with different purposes, and different languages. Above all this diversity, however, the Bible is unified by God's message that He is redeeming His creation and He is worthy of our faith. The Bible, like Jesus Christ, has a two-fold nature: it is both fully human and fully divine. In the Bible, some vast periods of time are passed over while others are recorded in detail. But as we read any of the books of the Bible, we are reading what the Holy Spirit selected as it relates to redemption. The Bible gives us the works and words of God, which show us both the immeasurable grace of God and the overwhelming need for us to respond to His grace with faith. Grace, as revealed in the Bible, is "God doing it." Faith is "our response to God doing it." The history of redemption shows us how God has done for us what we could never have done for ourselves. Clearly, the wrong response to God's redemptive activity is to try to save ourselves. The right response is to recognize our desperate need for God's grace, and humbly receive it through faith.

In this study we will seek to understand what God has done and spoken in human history. The focus of this study will be on the mighty acts and promises of God through which he prepared the world for Jesus Christ, provided redemption for humanity through Christ, and guaranteed the completion of His eternal plan in the future through Christ's reign on earth.

ACT ONE

God builds a nation
as His channel for
providing redemption.

Genesis 12 – 1 Kings 10

Setting the Stage:
The Pre-patriarchal Era (Genesis 1-11)

The Bible begins with the story of God creating the stage on which
the epic drama of redemption would be performed. Through His
omnipotent Word, the LORD God transformed what was formless
and empty into a beautiful world of light, land, and life. At the
pinnacle of His creation, He created human beings, male and
female, in His own image. And the LORD God blessed the man and
woman, placing them in the garden that He had made for them to
manage and enjoy. And God called His creation "very good."

Gen. 1

The goodness of creation included the tree of the knowledge of
good and evil. Presumably, the goodness of the tree and its
forbidden fruit was in its purpose for teaching Adam and Eve the
indispensible virtue of humble obedience to the voice of the LORD
God, without which no person can experience true and complete
goodness. True goodness is being with God, in His will, living in
line with His infinitely good nature. Adam and Eve experienced this
in the Garden of Eden.

Gen. 2

Onto the stage of this good creation entered a sinister being
described in Genesis 3 as "the serpent." This serpent, later known
as Satan, convinced Eve that God was withholding something from
her. And so she ate the forbidden fruit, pursuing the hidden
knowledge it would provide. Adam listened to Eve and ate the fruit
as well. By choosing their own desires above God's and pursuing
wisdom apart from God, Adam and Eve broke fellowship with their
Creator.

Gen. 3

God pronounced painful consequences on the serpent, Adam
and Eve, and on the ground. At the same time, He also gave the
first promise of the coming Redeemer. Genesis 3:15 records the
LORD's words to the serpent:

> *"And I will put enmity between thee and the woman, and
> between thy seed and her seed; he shall bruise thy head, and
> thou shalt bruise his heel." –Gen. 3:15*

This message of hope in a single male descendant is the first time
the LORD spoke of a coming solution to the Fall. As we will see
throughout the history of redemption, God often delivers His
greatest promises after humanity's most devastating failures.

In Genesis 1-11, the world faced three great crises, great times of need. The first crisis, as reviewed above, was the Fall. The second was the Flood, and the third was the Tower of Babel. In each of these crises God enacted His salvation and gave a promise.

Gen. 6   As Adam and Eve's descendants multiplied, so did the corruption of sin. Some of the saddest words in the Bible are recorded in Genesis 6:5-6, when the LORD looked at the world He created, now full of wickedness and violence, and declared:

> *"I will destroy man whom I have created from the face of the earth; both man, and beast, and the creeping thing, and the fowls of the air; for it repenteth me that I have made them." –*
> *Gen. 6:5-6*

But instead of eliminating all human and animal life from the earth, God gave grace to one man and his family. Genesis 6:8 beautifully states:

> *"But Noah found grace in the eyes of the LORD." –Gen. 6:8*

The story of Noah's ark is one of the earliest and most profound examples of God's grace in the history of redemption. By grace, God provided a way for Noah and his family to be protected from the judgment of the flood. And by grace, God made a way to redeem a small remnant of believers who would personally witness His faithfulness to His promises.

Gen. 8   When the floodwaters dried up and the ark came to rest, God followed his act of redemption with a great command and a great promise. In the history of redemption, when the LORD gives a word of command, it is always based on something God has done for the people He is addressing. And His commands are usually followed with great promises of hope for those who respond to His grace with obedience. This pattern of GRACE-COMMAND-PROMISE is an important key to understanding the works and words of God in the Bible.

Gen. 9   After delivering Noah and his family from the Flood, the LORD commanded them to multiply and replenish the earth, mirroring the command given to Adam and Eve in Gen. 1:22, 28. This is also the point where the LORD instituted the penalty of death for anyone who murdered another person (Gen. 9:6). Since human beings were God's representatives on earth, the taking of human life deserved the ultimate penalty. And using the sign of the rainbow as a perpetual reminder of His promise, the LORD vowed never to repeat his previous judgments—neither the curse on the ground (Gen. 3) nor the destruction of all animals and humans by a worldwide flood (Gen. 6-9). In addition to this promise, the LORD gave Noah a prophecy concerning his three sons. In Noah's prophecy, the LORD revealed a message of hope with the words in Gen. 9:26-27, "Blessed be the LORD God of Shem...He [God] shall dwell in the tents of Shem." And so, Shem would be the one through whom the "seed" promised earlier (Gen. 3:15) would come.

The third crisis of humanity again resulted from blatant disobedience to God's will. Gen. 11 reveals that Noah's descendants, *Gen. 11* whose population had grown to large numbers, deliberately resisted God's command to scatter and replenish the earth saying:

> *"Let us build us a city and a tower, whose top may reach unto heaven; and let us make us a name, lest we be scattered abroad upon the face of the whole earth." –Gen. 11:4*

Their pride and drive for personal glory was a direct affront to God's plan to fill the earth with His glory. God's desire was for humankind to multiply and spread across the earth and exercise dominion over it, under the authority of God. In the same way as Eve pursued wisdom without God, these people were abandoning their Maker in pursuit of self-sufficiency. But, being true to His promise, the LORD did not repeat His previous judgments, choosing instead to scatter the people by breaking down their ability to communicate with each other (Gen. 11:7-8). Their building project- a temple to human autonomy- was left forever unfinished.

The judgment at Babel teaches, for a third time in Genesis 1-11, that all human effort apart from God comes to nothing. The pride that underlies such attempts always leads to judgment. Without God we will perish in the waters of judgment; we are hopelessly lost without His saving intervention.

From the fragmented civilization that sprung from the scattering at Babel, God was about to issue His clearest promise of redemption. It was a promise which climaxed all of the blessings which came before it. And it would be given, as it should be expected, to a descendant of Shem.

Scene One:
The Drama Begins (Genesis 12-29)

Gen. 12

While Genesis 1-11 deals with the whole world, the focus of Genesis 12-50 is basically on one man and his family. The main characters are Abram (later called Abraham), his son Isaac, his grandson Jacob, and his great-grandson Joseph.

Abram, a descendant of Shem, became the recipient of God's covenant promise, as recorded in Genesis 12:1-3:

"And I will make of thee a great nation, and I will bless thee, and make thy name great; and thou shalt be a blessing: And I will bless them that bless thee, and curse him that curseth thee: and in thee shall all families of the earth be blessed." –Gen. 12:2-3

In this covenant promise to Abram, the LORD presented the blueprint of His plan. Starting with one man, He would build a great nation. And in this one man and his descendants, all the families of the earth would find God's blessing. The promise to Abram is the key to understanding the nation of Israel and its role in the history of redemption. Israel was chosen and created by God as the channel through which God's blessing would come to the world. No other ancient writings contain any such promise of blessing for the whole earth. The history of Israel is the history of a people in a special relationship with God and the ancestry of the Redeemer of humanity.

When Christ the Redeemer came, He initiated the fulfillment of God's promise that all the families would be blessed through Abraham when he proclaimed:

"All power is given unto me in heaven and in earth. Go ye therefore, and teach all nations, baptizing them in the name of the Father, and of the Son, and of the Holy Ghost: Teaching them to observe all things whatsoever I have commanded you: and, lo, I am with you alway, even unto the end of the world." – Matt. 28:18-20

Jesus' guarantee in Matt. 16:18, "I will build My church" parallels the LORD's promise to Abraham, "I will make of thee a great nation." While the nation of Israel was created in *anticipation* of the Savior who would come, the Church would be created through the *proclamation* of the Savior who had come.

Following the scattering at Babel, the LORD started to create a nation, beginning with Abram. Three major elements are necessary to establish a nation as an official entity. A nation is comprised of (1) a common people, (2) a common government with laws and leadership, and (3) a common land. The following chart gives a preview of how the LORD brought these three elements together to create the nation of Israel:

The Establishment of the Nation of Israel		
Key Element	**Key Historical Event(s)**	**Key Passage(s)**
A common people	Abram's family grows from one son to millions of people in Egypt	Gen. 12—Ex. 3
A common government	Moses becomes the leader and the Law (their constitution) is given at Sinai	Ex. 3—Deut. 34
A common land	Israel conquers the land of Canaan under Joshua's leadership	Joshua

After reading the LORD's promise to Abram in Gen. 12:1-3, one might expect the following passages (Gen. 12:4—20:18) to record a flourishing family tree and a grandiose posterity for Abram. *Gen. 16* Instead, the reader is surprised to find that Abram was in no way a natural candidate to become the father of a great nation. He was already seventy-five years old at the time he received the promise. His wife Sarai was sixty-five and had never been able to conceive a child. Even ten years after receiving the message that he would become the father of a great nation, Abram was childless. After waiting for ten years without conceiving a child, Abram and Sarai took the matter into their own hands and tried to do what God said He would do. Following Sarai's suggestion, Abram fathered a son by Hagar, Sarai's handmaid (Gen. 16:1-3). The child's name was Ishmael, and although God promised to care for him and bless him, he was not the child through whom God's plan of redemption would be carried forward.

Gen. 17   Another 14 years passed before the LORD appeared again to Abram (Gen. 17:1-27). This time, the LORD declared that Abram's name would be changed from "Exalted Father" (Abram) to "Father of a Multitude" (Abraham). Both names appeared strange for a man who was 99 years old with no children. Abraham's wife's name was also changed from Sarai to Sarah. While the meaning of Abraham's name changed slightly, the meaning of Sarah's name did not change at all. This probably indicates that it was the change of identity that was most important for Abraham and Sarah rather than the names themselves. Their identity was now defined in terms of their participation in God's plan of redemption, using names that were given to them by the God of promise Himself. This might cause each of us to wonder, "How is my name associated with God's plan of redemption?"

Gen. 21   One year after "the great name change" the LORD fulfilled His promise when Sarah gave birth to a son. Abraham and Sarah called him Isaac, meaning "laughter", a name that recalled their reaction when they were given a promise that seemed too amazing to be true: the impossible promise of having a child in their old age (Gen. 17:17; 18:12). Through the birth of Isaac, God confirmed that His plan of redemption did not depend on Abraham and Sarah's planning and effort. It was God Himself who was going to build the nation. And, as summarized in Heb. 11:8-12, Abraham and Sarah finally understood that their role was simply to respond to God's promises in faith; to trust God's word and participate in His plan as He prescribed. Through faith they inherited the promises of God.

Gen. 22   When Isaac was grown, the LORD tested Abraham at an entirely new level of difficulty. The LORD commanded Abraham to take the son of promise, Isaac, and offer him as a burnt offering. Imagine Abraham's confusion! Had God not promised that it was Isaac, and no other son, through whom the great nation would be built? If the command to sacrifice Isaac was not from God, Abraham would be guilty of the most horrific murder imaginable— the killing of his miraculous son of promise. Hebrews 11:17-19 gives the key to understanding Abraham's willingness to obey God's command and the basis for his faith: Abraham believed that God would raise Isaac from the dead (Gen. 22:5). Abraham also knew that if God commanded a burnt offering, He would provide the means for it (Gen. 22:8). As Romans 4:21 states, Abraham was "fully persuaded" that God would not break His promise. And God had emphatically stated that Isaac was the key to the fulfillment of God's promises (Gen. 17:21). As Abraham's knife was about to fall on the son he loved, God provided a ram to take Isaac's place on the altar. Through God's testing of Abraham, He figuratively demonstrated the resurrection and the substitutionary sacrifice that the coming Redeemer would provide when Isaac, doomed to death on the altar, was delivered because of the ram that God provided to take his place. And through Abraham's faith, He gave Isaac and all of his descendants an example of pure faith. For Abraham trusted God; and Abraham obeyed God. He trusted God because God had kept his promise of giving Abraham a son despite how impossible it seemed. And He obeyed God because He trusted Him. If he refused to obey God, he would keep Isaac, but at what cost? How could any blessing be worth breaking his relationship with the Promise-keeping God? This kind of fear—loving fear—is what the LORD rewarded in Abraham (Gen. 22:12-18). We can each identify with Abraham, because we know the fear we feel when we do not know what the future holds. Yet now, in the present, we have God's Word as our reason to believe in His goodness, power, and omniscience. And therefore we can trust and obey Him.

Parallels between Mt. Moriah and Mt. Calvary		
Scripture	**Mt. Moriah**	**Mt. Calvary**
Gen. 22:2	*"Take now thy son,*	*"God...hath spoken to us by His Son." Heb. 1:2*
	Thine only son,	*"God...gave His only begotten Son." Jn. 3:16*
	Whom thou lovest.	*"The only begotten Son, which is in the bosom of the Father." Jn. 1:18*
	And get thee into the land of Moriah,	*"Solomon began to build the house of the Lord...in Mount Moriah." (This was probably the same place of the temple sacrifices.) 2 Chron. 3:1*

	upon one of the mountains that I will tell thee of.	*"And when they were come to the place which is called Calvary, there they crucified Him."* —Luke 23:33
	And offer him there for a burnt offering."	*"Sanctified through the offering of the body of Jesus Christ once for all." —Heb. 10:5-10*
Gen. 22:4	*"Abraham lifted up his eyes and saw the place afar off."*	*"God before hath showed by the mouth of all His prophets that Christ should suffer." (The Father knew before the foundation of the world.) —Acts 3:18*
Gen. 22:6	*"And Abraham took the wood of the burnt offering, and laid it upon Isaac his son. And they went both of them together."*	*And He, bearing His cross, went forth. — Jn. 19:17; John 18:11* *"Therefore doth My Father love Me, because I lay down My life. No man taketh it from Me, but I lay it down of Myself. This commandment have I received of My Father." —Jn. 10:17, 18*
Gen. 22:7	*"Where is the lamb for a burnt offering?"*	*"Behold the Lamb of God which taketh away the sin of the world." —Jn. 1:29*

Gen. 22:8	"God will provide Himself the Lamb. So they went both of them together."	"The Lamb slain from the foundation of the world." —Rev. 13:8
Gen. 22:9	"Abraham built an altar there, and bound Isaac his son, and laid him upon the altar upon the wood."	"I delight to do Thy will, O My God." —Ps. 40:8 "Him being delivered by the determinate counsel and foreknowledge of God." —Acts 2:23 "The Lord hath laid on Him the iniquity of us all." —Isa. 53:6
Gen. 22:10	"And Abraham stretched forth his hand and took the knife to slay his son."	"It pleased the Lord to bruise Him." —Isa. 53:10 "My God, My God, why hast Thou forsaken Me?" —Mt. 27:46
Gen. 22:11	"The angel of the Lord called unto him out of heaven."	Contrast. (No voice from heaven.) He saved others, Himself He cannot save. —Mt. 26:53, 54; Mt. 27:42
Gen. 22:12	"Thou hast not withheld thy son, thine only son."	(When God speaks of deep grief He compares it to the loss of an only son.) —Jer. 6:26
Gen. 22:13	"Abraham took the ram, and offered him up for a burnt offering in the stead of his son."	"He is brought as a lamb to the slaughter...He shall bear their iniquities." —Isa. 53:7, 11

Gen. 26 Abraham was not the only recipient of God's Promise. The LORD appeared to Isaac when he was in the land of the Philistines (part of the Promised Land), assuring him:

> *"Sojourn in this land, and I will be with thee, and will bless thee; for unto thee, and unto thy seed, I will give all these countries, and I will perform the oath which I sware unto Abraham thy father; And I will make thy seed to multiply as the stars of heaven, and will give unto thy seed all these countries; and in thy seed shall all the nations of the earth be blessed;" –Gen. 26:3-4*

The LORD did not leave Isaac to wander through life aimlessly as only a passive instrument for God's redemption. The LORD revealed Himself personally to Isaac, demonstrating that He would be faithful to Isaac just as He had been to his father Abraham. Isaac's wife Rebekah, like Sarah, was unable to have children. But, as Gen. 25:21 records, Isaac pleaded with the LORD who listened and gave her twin boys, Jacob and Esau. This was eighty-five years after the first time the LORD promised a son to Abraham.

Gen. 28 Although the LORD promised Esau a heritage (Deut. 2:5), he was not the one to carry on God's plan of redemption. Jacob was the next recipient of the Promise. Gen. 28:13-15 describes the LORD standing at the top of a stairway to heaven, giving His personal promise to Jacob:

> *"And, behold, the LORD stood above it, and said, I am the LORD God of Abraham thy father, and the God of Isaac: the land whereon thou liest, to thee will I give it, and to thy seed; And thy seed shall be as the dust of the earth, and thou shalt spread abroad to the west, and to the east, and to the north, and to the south: and in thee and in thy seed shall all the families of the earth be blessed. And, behold, I am with thee, and will keep thee in all places whither thou goest, and will bring thee again into this land; for I will not leave thee, until I have done that which I have spoken to thee of." –Gen. 28:13-15*

Jacob's wife Rachel was barren. Again, the LORD answered prayer and enabled Rachel to have two sons, Joseph and Benjamin. Jacob was faced with the same challenge to his faith as his father and grandfather, and like them, he saw the LORD keep His Promise in spite of discouraging circumstances.

The LORD honored the three patriarchs, Abraham, Isaac, and Jacob as the founders of His nation. And through them, He established Himself as the personal, promise-keeping God. In several passages in both the Old and New Testaments, the LORD describes Himself as, "The God of Abraham, Isaac, and Jacob" (Gen. 50:24; 2 Kings 13:23; Matt. 8:11, 22:32). He had personally given His Promise to these three men and confirmed His words by His miraculous acts on their behalf. Each of these men had wives who could not have had a single child, yet through them the LORD was laying the foundation for His nation.

You may be asking yourself, "Why would God choose barren women to begin building His nation?" Paul answered this question in his first letter to the believers in Corinth:

"...so that no human being might boast in the presence of God...as it is written, 'Let the one who boasts, boast in the Lord.'"
–1 Cor.1:29-31

Abraham's Seven "Separations" in Genesis	
12:1	From his culture and country
12:2	From his kindred and his old associations
13:1	From Egypt
13:11	From selfishness or carnality (Lot)
14:21	From ill-gotten gain
17:18	From man-made attempts (Hagar)
22:12f	From loving God's gift above God Himself (Isaac)

God Speaks: The Promise to Abraham
(Genesis 12-22)

God's first word to Abraham was a unilateral covenant based on His gracious promise. The only condition necessary for Abraham to experience the blessings God promised was faith—that he trust God and obey His command to leave his country. This command, however, was not a way for Abraham to earn or merit God's blessings. As further explained below, God's promised plan was the reason for Abraham to leave his country, and Abraham's trusting obedience was the response by which he would receive the blessings and be the blessing God promised.

The Need: As seen in Genesis 1-11, mankind is alienated from God because of his sin. He is a sinner both by nature and by choice. The great need of mankind is to be reconciled with God and have a relationship with Him. To obtain this relationship, Abraham needed to know God's gracious plan for Him as the basis for his faith in God. Amos 3:7 states, "Surely the Lord GOD does nothing, unless He reveals His secret to His servants the prophets" (NKJV). And Romans 10:17 says, "So then faith comes by hearing, and hearing by the word of God" (NKJV).

The Content: God speaks concerning what He will do for Abraham. God gives His promise to Abraham in various stages of development, found in Genesis 12:1-3, 7; 12:14-16; 15:4-21; 17:4-16; and 22:15-18. A study of these passages reveals a progressive expansion of the three basis elements of the promise: (1) descendants (or "seed"), (2) a land, and (3) a blessing to all the families of the earth. Throughout these passages, God continually says, "I will." This teaches a crucial lesson about God's grace: grace is *God doing it!*

The Method: God spoke to Abraham using a vision (Gen. 15) and directly in spoken words. According to James 2:23, God spoke to Abraham as a friend. This method is appropriate for what God was speaking about. When we are going to do something for another person, we speak to them as a friend.

The Response Required: The wrong response to God's promise, exhibited by Abraham in Genesis 16:1-4, is trying, in our own wisdom and strength, to do what God said He would do in His wisdom and strength. False teachers often promote salvation by *works*, while the true believer responds in faith to God's *grace* (Eph. 2:8). The right response, then, is faith—the trust (waiting and expecting God to do it) and obedience demonstrated by Abraham in Genesis 22:1-22. Some important New Testament passages on "the right response" are James 4:17, which shows the obedience of faith; Romans 4:13-25, the New Testament abstract of faith, and Hebrews 10:25-12:2, an explanation of the right response toward God's Word.

Scene Two:
The Tribal Framework (Genesis 30-50)

So far, the common people who would form God's chosen nation had not experienced any thing close to the large-scale growth God had promised Abraham. After the first two generations (Abraham and Isaac) there was still only one descendant: Jacob. There had to be a larger structure upon which to build the nation. To solve this problem, the LORD gave Jacob twelve sons who would form the state framework for the nation—the twelve tribes of Israel.

Gen. 30

The twelve sons, in the order of their birth, were Reuben, Simeon, Levi, Judah, Dan, Naphtali, Gad, Asher, Issachar, Zebulun, Joseph and Benjamin. In all, Jacob's clan grew to seventy members living with him in the Promised Land.

Genesis 30-50 begins by recording the growth of Jacob's family in the Promised Land and ends with all of Jacob's family moving to Egypt to escape a famine in their homeland.

Through an unpredictable series of events, Jacob's son Joseph became the preserver of God's people, despite the personal injustice he suffered from his brothers and the Egyptians. When he was reunited with his family in Egypt, Joseph looked back on his life and the wrong his brothers had done to him:

Gen. 45

> *"Now therefore be not grieved, nor angry with yourselves, that ye sold me hither: for God did send me before you to preserve life. For these two years hath the famine been in the land: and yet there are five years, in the which there shall neither be earing nor harvest. And God sent me before you to preserve you a posterity in the earth, and to save your lives by a great deliverance. So now it was not you that sent me hither, but God: and he hath made me a father to Pharaoh, and lord of all his house, and a ruler throughout all the land of Egypt." –Gen. 45:5-8*

How essential it is for us to see our own history in the light of God's plan of redemption, in order to say, like Joseph, "but God!"

Gen. 50

In addition to his role as the preserver of God's chosen people, Joseph also knew God's faithfulness to His Promise. At the end of his life, Joseph assured his family that they would not live in Egypt forever.

"And Joseph said unto his brethren, I die: and God will surely visit you, and bring you out of this land unto the land which he sware to Abraham, to Isaac, and to Jacob. And Joseph took an oath of the children of Israel, saying, God will surely visit you, and ye shall carry up my bones from hence." –Gen. 50:24-25

The LORD would return His people to the land He had promised them. But the land was only one of the three elements needed to establish the nation. At Joseph's death, Abraham's descendants were merely a few common people living under a foreign government. For the moment, in the safety of a temporary setting in Egypt, the LORD was forming the population of His nation.

Scene Three:
The Common People (Exodus 1)

Joseph arranged for the seventy members of his family to live in
Egypt working as shepherds in a region called Goshen. Ex. 1:7   *Ex. 1*
describes how the LORD developed the population of His nation in
Egypt:

> *"And the children of Israel were fruitful, and increased
> abundantly, and multiplied, and waxed exceeding mighty; and
> the land was filled with them." –Ex. 1:7*

The Israelites lived and multiplied in Egypt for almost 400 years.
As their numbers grew, the Egyptians began to see them as a threat,
fearing that the Israelites might fight against them in the event of
an invasion by a foreign power. The Egyptians pursued two
solutions to the Israelite threat: oppression and infanticide.

First, they put the Israelites to work on public projects, forcing
them to perform all of the harshest labor under heavy-handed
supervision. They made bricks and mortar, worked in the field, and
performed all kinds of manual labor. The Egyptians reasoned that if
they kept the Israelites under enough oppression, they would have
no strength left for insubordination.

The second measure used against the Israelites was infanticide.
The Pharaoh commanded the Israelites to kill all their male
children at birth. The midwives did not comply with the Pharaoh's
command, and the LORD continued to multiply His people. The
Egyptians were unable to stop what the LORD was doing (Ex. 1:8-
20).

So, for nearly 400 years, Israel's (formerly called Jacob)
descendants lived in Egypt, working as slaves, making bricks, and
having babies.

The LORD had finally created a common people, probably
more than two million in population[3], but they were living as slaves
in Egypt. They had no means of governing themselves, and no land
of their own. Remember the three key elements of a nation: (1) a
people with a language, (2) leadership and laws, and (3) a
homeland.

---

[3] Based on the numbers of fighting men in Numbers 1 and Exodus 38:25-26.

Scene Four:
The Leader (Exodus 2-4)

Ex. 2

The LORD created a leader for Israel by raising him from birth and orchestrating the events of his life to shape him into an effective leader. Moses was born to Israelite parents who were faced with Pharaoh's orders to drown their newborn baby boy in the river. Once she could no longer hide Moses, his mother placed him in a floating basket which she hoped would carry him to safety as he floated down the river. Pharaoh's daughter found the basket, and Moses, God's leader, was raised as a prince in the household of the same king that ordered his death.

God provided initial training for His leader using a pagan nation. As an Egyptian prince, Moses' education probably included athletics, art, writing, music, geometry, literature, law, astronomy, medicine and philosophy. He could have chosen a career in politics, business, literature, or in the military.

But Moses' Egyptian education did not sufficiently prepare him to become the leader of God's people. When he was forty years old, he saw an Egyptian taskmaster beating one of his fellow Israelites. Moses killed the Egyptian and tried to conceal what he had done by burying the man's body in the sand. Later, Moses tried to settle a dispute between two Israelites. But the men refused to recognize his leadership (Ex. 2:11-15; cf. Acts 7:23-29). Although Moses had the desire to help his people, he asserted himself instead of acting in God's timing. Knowing that his murder of the Egyptian taskmaster would be discovered, Moses fled across the desert to the land of Midian. In Midian, Moses' identity as a prince of Egypt evaporated. He became a shepherd, settling down to an anonymous life on the back side of the desert with a wife and two sons.

Ex. 3

By the time the LORD appeared to Moses in the burning bush on Mount Sinai (Ex. 3:6-8), Moses had lived in Midian for forty years. He was no longer the strong-willed, assertive young man that killed the Egyptian and confronted the quarrelling Israelites. When the LORD called him to lead, Moses was reluctant; he responded with self-doubt. He said, "Who am I?" (Ex. 3:11-12), "What shall I say?" (Ex. 3:13-14), "They will not believe" (Ex. 4:1-2), and "I am not eloquent" (Ex. 4:10). If Moses was ever going to lead God's people out of slavery, his confidence would have to be in the LORD alone. His self-confidence had vanished. This was the leader the LORD wanted—a man who would humbly depend on Him, trust Him, and follow His will.

Moses' life can be summarized as follows:

i)   Forty years as a dignitary in Egypt
ii) Forty years as a desert shepherd in Midian
iii) Forty years as a deliverer of Israel

Moses held a unique position as the leader of Israel. He was
their deliverer, lawgiver, builder, commander-in-chief, judge,   *Ex. 4*
author and intermediary between the people and God. No one
except the Son of God Himself ever fulfilled a broader range of
leadership functions.

Already, the Israelites had become a common people. In Moses,
they now had a leader. But they could never be their own nation as
long as they were under the government of Egypt. In order for them
to be set apart and begin to function as God's nation they had to be
delivered from their Egyptian oppressors.

Scene Five:
Deliverance from Egypt (Exodus 5-19)

The Israelites' sojourn in Egypt was part of God's plan of redemption from the beginning. The LORD had informed Abraham in advance of what would take place.

> "Know of a surety that thy seed shall be a stranger in a land that is not theirs, and shall serve them; and they shall afflict them four hundred years; And also that nation, whom they shall serve, will I judge: and afterward shall they come out with great substance." –Gen. 15:13-14

When the LORD appeared to Moses in the burning bush on Mount Sinai, the 400 years were complete. The LORD was about to deliver His people from their affliction.

When Moses returned to Egypt he arrived with his brother Aaron whom the LORD had appointed as Moses' spokesperson. Aaron spoke the words of the LORD to the people while Moses performed the signs the LORD had commanded him to do before the Israelites. In contrast to his first attempt to take leadership by his own initiative, Moses was now empowered by the LORD Himself. And this time, the people believed (Ex. 4:31).

Ex. 5
Ex. 5 records the beginning of the process that led to Israel's deliverance from Egypt. Moses and Aaron formally requested that Pharaoh allow the Israelites to leave Egypt in order to obey the command of the LORD. Pharaoh refused, accusing the Israelites of laziness and ordering their work to be made even more rigorous than it already was. His ludicrous demand for harder labor intensified the situation and accelerated it toward a breaking point.

Ex. 6
Both the people and Moses became confused and frustrated. The LORD had promised them deliverance, yet it seemed more impossible than ever. They had trusted God, but nothing had happened. When Moses returned to pray to the LORD, he plainly and honestly laid out his distress before Him. The LORD answered with a powerful promise:

> "Wherefore say unto the children of Israel, I am the LORD, and I will bring you out from under the burdens of the Egyptians, and I will rid you out of their bondage, and I will redeem you with a stretched out arm, and with great judgments: And I will take you to me for a people, and I will be to you a God: and ye shall know that I am the LORD your God, which bringeth you out

from under the burdens of the Egyptians. And I will bring you in unto the land, concerning the which I did swear to give it to Abraham, to Isaac, and to Jacob; and I will give it you for an heritage: I am the LORD." –Ex.6:6-8

Moses repeatedly declared the words of the LORD to Pharaoh: "Let My people go." Time after time Pharaoh initially agreed, but subsequently refused to allow them to leave. With each refusal, Pharaoh brought a judgment from God upon himself and his people. These miraculous events were intended to convince Pharaoh that the LORD had indeed spoken and ought to be feared and obeyed.[4] God unleashed his awesome power in ten signs of judgment against the Egyptians and their false gods (Ex. 7-12):

Ex. 7

The Ten Plagues	
Water into blood	Boils and sores
Frogs	Hail and fire
Lice or gnats	Locusts
Flies	Three days of darkness
Death of cattle	Death of the firstborn

The plagues attacked numerous objects of Egyptian worship, showing how powerless they really were:

Objects of Egyptian Worship	
The Nile River	The Bull
The Frog	The Atmosphere
The Earth	The Sun
The Scarab Beetle	Pharaoh himself

---

[4] Kaiser, *The Promise-Plan of God*, 72.

Ex. 12   The last of the plagues was a divinely-instituted ritual that prefigured the sacrifice of the coming Redeemer. The Passover served two functions: (1) to protect the believing Israelites from God's judgment on the Egyptians and (2) to illustrate God's redemptive solution for the world. The Passover became the most sacred and meaningful ritual the Israelites observed. It demonstrated the principle that a perfect sacrifice was the only means of salvation from death. The answer for humanity's great need for salvation would be Jesus Christ, the Savior. He would voluntarily give His own life as the sacrifice for the sins of the world. Notice the similarities between the Passover and the events surrounding the death of Jesus Christ:

Christ's Fulfillment of Passover	
Passover	**Christ**
The sacrifice must be a lamb (Ex. 12:3).	Christ was the Lamb of God (1 Cor. 5:7).
The lamb must be without spot (Ex. 12:5).	Christ was without spot or blemish (1 Pet. 1:18-19).
The lamb's blood was shed that Israel might have life (Ex. 12:23).	Christ's Blood was shed that men might have life (Jn. 3:16).

Ex. 15   The LORD had promised He would redeem the Israelites from their bondage in Egypt (Ex. 6:6). Ex. 12:31—15:27 records how the LORD delivered his chosen people using powerful signs and wonders. This redemption was the fundamental act of God which gave the Israelites their identity as a nation. He had promised to make a great nation from Abraham, and now he had delivered His people, freeing them to worship Him and experience His blessing.

Scene Six:
The Nation's Constitution (Exodus 20)

Having been delivered from oppressive slavery in Egypt, the Israelites found themselves in need of their own government. They had a God-given leader in Moses, but they had no written document to define their identity and set forth their guiding principles. For this reason the Law was given to Moses and Israel at Mt. Sinai (Ex. 19ff). In the Law, the LORD graciously provided his people with moral, ceremonial, and civil guidance. The moral aspect of the Law was rooted in God's own holy nature (Ex. 20:2), which provided the standard for all of the nation's ethical decisions and actions. With His own perfect holiness as the fixed standard, and knowing the frailty of the people He redeemed, the LORD also provided the ceremonial aspects of the Law for those moments when the people failed to live up to His perfect standard. Although these ceremonial observances did not in themselves provide the solution for sin, they were designed to point forward to God's own perfect and final sacrifice for the sin of all humanity—His Son. The LORD unified the people and focused their worship around the tabernacle, where He would manifest His presence at the center of His people. The civil commands in the Law were applications of the moral law to the specific situations the Israelite community faced during the Mosaic era.

Ex. 20

It is important to notice that God's commands, which He delivered in the form of the Law given to Moses, were entirely based on what He had done for the people. The commandments were intended to direct the people's response to God, not as a means by which they would earn God's favor. He had already given them His favor without any merit on their part. The LORD had delivered His people from slavery so that His glory could be displayed in redemption. And, in giving the Law, the LORD was instructing His people on how to live as a holy nation set apart for a dual purpose: first, to be an example of God's own holiness and second, to be the channel for God's redemptive purpose as He carried it forward. No other nation had a constitution like Israel's:

> *"For what great nation is there that has a god so near to it as the Lord our God is to us, whenever we call upon him? And what great nation is there, that has statutes and rules so righteous as all this law that I set before you today?" –Deut. 4:7-8*

God Speaks: The Mosaic Law
(Exodus 19-40; Leviticus; Deuteronomy)

God spoke to Moses 439 years after His promise to Abraham. He gave the Law after redeeming them from Egypt (Ex. 6:6-7). The Israelites did not have to keep the law in order to be delivered; the Law was God's guidance for the people he redeemed.

The Need: God has a multitude of people on their way to the promised land, and they need direction. People, including Christians, tend to have a bad taste for law, but this is probably because they do not understand the purpose for which God gave it. As an example, parents must tell a child what they want him or her to know (what is right, what is wrong, what the limits are, what the consequences are for disobedience, etc.). At this point in biblical history, God is building a nation. Nations must have laws in order for people to govern themselves. In the Law, God is saying, "This is what I would like you to be." Some Christians often repeat, "We are not under law." Christians are not under the laws given to Old Testament Israel, but 1 Corinthians 9:21 states that we are *"under law to Christ."* While the specific civil and ceremonial laws of Israel have served their purpose, the moral law of God still shows all people, created in God's own image, that we need to act like God!

The Content: The first aspect of the Law was the moral law, expressed in the Ten Commandments (Ex. 20:1-17). The moral law covers every aspect of life: our relationship to God, our worship, and our relationship to each other in society. It addresses how we ought to live, act and respond to God. The central message of the moral law, as given to Israel, is captured in Lev. 19:2, "You shall be holy, for I the LORD your God am holy." The second aspect of the Mosaic Law was the ceremonial law (Ex. 25:1-8; 28:1; 29:38-46). Based on the pattern of its heavenly reality (Ex. 25:40; Acts 7:44), it instructed the nation on how to respond to God in worship, providing a place (the Tabernacle), rituals, priests, methods of cleansing, and sacrifices for sin which pointed forward to their ultimate fulfillment in the Messiah. Through the sacrificial system, the people demonstrated their faith in God and that they understood their need for forgiveness. The Mosaic Law had its roots even earlier, in God's words to Abraham, "I am Almighty God; walk before Me and be blameless" (Gen. 17:1, NKJV).

The Method: The LORD spoke using thunder, lightning, clouds, trumpet blasts, smoke, fire, and an earthquake, engraving His words on stone tablets. (Ex. 19:16-25; 20:18-21). This method caused the people to be too afraid to approach the LORD. Only Moses, whom the LORD called, went up to the mountain.

The Response Required: The correct response is to obey (Ex. 19:5-8); a personal commitment, by free choice, to God and what He says. After hearing the Law, the people of Israel responded, "All the words that the LORD has said we will do" (Ex. 24:3, NKJV).

Scene Seven:
The Nation's Homeland (Numbers, Deuteronomy, and Joshua)

After receiving the Law at Mount Sinai, Israel's identity was two-thirds complete. They were a common people with a common government. They had been delivered from Egypt and they had a leader, a constitution and laws. But they still lacked the final element in their formation: a national homeland.

By the end of their 400-year sojourn in Egypt, Israel's population had grown from about seventy to an astounding number of people, probably more than two million.[5] Since the desert could not sustain such a massive population, the LORD miraculously provided for His people's needs (Num. 11). Let us never doubt God's ability or willingness to provide "a table in the wilderness" for His people!

Num. 11

The LORD was leading the Israelites back to the land of Canaan—the land that was promised to Abraham, Isaac and Jacob where they had raised their families. The land of Canaan was both the land of Israel's heritage and their Promised Land. They arrived at the border of the land and decided to send spies ahead of them to plan their conquest. Initially, the Israelites sent out the twelve spies in order to determine *how* they would conquer the land, not to help them decide *if* they would take it over. Numbers 13-36 records the sad history of the Israelites' failure to trust God and enter the Promised Land.

Israel's Failure to Enter the Promised Land		
Num. 13:1-2	The LORD commanded the spies to be sent out into Canaan.	They were to see *how*, not *if*, they were to conquer the land.
Num. 13:17-20	Moses gave the spies their orders.	They would verify what the LORD had promised.

---

5 Based on the numbers of fighting men in Numbers 1 and Exodus 38:25-26.

Num. 13:25-29	The spies brought back their report on the land.	They confirmed that the land was good, but despaired because of the giants.
Num. 14:1-3	The people despaired and rebelled.	They correctly saw their weakness, but they refused to trust the LORD.
Num. 14:5	Moses and Aaron prayed.	They "fell on their faces."
Num. 14:7-10	Joshua and Caleb tried to persuade the people.	They demonstrated their faith in God.
Num. 14:11-19	The LORD was about to destroy the people and start over with Moses, who interceded for them.	After all they had seen the LORD do for them, the people still refused to trust Him. Moses appealed to the LORD's glory.
Num. 14:20-23	The LORD set aside those who refused to trust Him.	Those who rebelled did not receive what God promised, but the Promise was passed on.
Num. 14:39-45	The LORD judged the Israelites.	He was not with them when they went to battle.

Psalm 106:24-27 summarizes what God did because of the Israelites' unbelief:

> *"Yea, they despised the pleasant land, they believed not his word:*
> *But murmured in their tents, and hearkened not unto the voice of*
> *the LORD. Therefore he lifted up his hand against them, to*
> *overthrow them in the wilderness: To overthrow their seed also*
> *among the nations, and to scatter them in the lands." —Psa.*
> *106:24-27*

Although most of the people of Israel failed to trust the LORD and enter the Promised Land, there were some who did trust the LORD. Caleb and Joshua lived to inherit the land that the LORD had promised, while those who turned away from the Promise perished in the wilderness. This illustrates another principle in the history of redemption: even if some refuse to take part in the fulfillment of God's promises, God will find someone who will.

The book of Hebrews uses the story of the Israelites in the wilderness as a warning to God's people:

> *"And with whom was He angry for forty years? Was it not with*
> *those who sinned, whose bodies fell in the wilderness? And to*
> *whom did He swear that they should not enter His rest, but to*
> *those who were disobedient? And so we see that they were not*
> *able to enter because of unbelief." —Heb. 3:17-19*

> *"Take care, brethren, lest there should be in any one of you an*
> *evil, unbelieving heart, in falling away from the living God." —*
> *Heb. 3:12*

Deuteronomy begins with the people of Israel at the border of the Promised Land for a second time. This time, after forty years in the wilderness, they would be sure not to make the same mistake as the previous generation did when they failed to trust the LORD to help them defeat the inhabitants of the Promised Land. Moses began by reviewing all of the great acts of God by which He brought the Israelites to where they were, on the verge of possessing the Promised Land. The LORD had already enabled the Israelites to defeat two mighty kings on the eastern side of the Jordan: Sihon, king of Heshbon and Og, king of Bashan. On the basis of God's great saving acts, Moses then delivered *Torah*—the instruction of God—showing the people the way to live as His chosen and holy people.

Deut. 1

The Israelites had spent forty years wandering in circles in the desert. Although the people were in the desert because of their unbelief, the LORD used this experience for more than punishment. Deuteronomy 8 describes how the LORD faithfully provided for his people throughout their long years in the

Deut. 8

wilderness. In the midst of judgment for their sin, the LORD was teaching and training His people to prepare them for the Promised Land and the fulfillment of the blessings He had promised. At the end of Deuteronomy, Moses died and Joshua became the new leader of the people of God.

Josh. 1   Before Joshua launched his attack on the kings of Canaan, the LORD came to him and personally assured him that He was going to keep His promises to Moses. The LORD directly commissioned Joshua to lead the people into the Promised Land, assuring him saying:

> *"Have not I commanded thee? Be strong and of a good courage;*
> *be not afraid, neither be thou dismayed: for the LORD thy God is*
> *with thee whithersoever thou goest." –Josh. 1:9*

As he had done for Abraham, Isaac, Jacob and Moses, the LORD also spoke directly to Joshua so that he could be sure that the LORD was with him.

As one reads through the book of Joshua, the account of Israel's conquest of the land of the Canaanites raises ethical questions: how is this violent conquest morally justified? Hundreds of years before the conquest, while Abraham was living in Canaan, the LORD promised him that his descendants would return there, "in the fourth generation" because, He said, "the iniquity of the Amorites is not yet complete" (Gen. 15:16). The Amorites were one of the Canaanite people groups who practiced moral abominations such as idolatry, bestiality, and child sacrifice (Lev. 18-19, esp. 18:24). In spite of their corruption, the LORD showed His mercy and longsuffering by giving these people four generations to repent and be spared (Jer. 18:7). And the LORD did not show special favoritism to Israel, either. When they corrupted themselves with the sins of the Canaanites, the LORD showed them longsuffering and mercy, but eventually His judgment came upon them just as it had come upon the Canaanites. Another nation came and took their land (see Act Two).

The Book of Joshua has three parts:

i)   The conquest of the land (1-12)
ii) The division of the land (13-21)
iii) Joshua's farewell addresses (22-24)

The Conquest of the Promised Land		
Josh. 1:1-5	The renewal of the Promise	Joshua was a servant before he was a leader.
Josh. 1:6-9	The conditions of the Promise	The people must trust and obey.
Josh. 5:13-14	The Commander of the LORD's army.	The LORD Himself would fight for them.
Josh. 6:1-3, 21	The thrill of victory	The walls of Jericho crashed down by the hand of God.
Josh. 7:1-5	The agony of defeat	The people suffered defeat at Ai because of Achan's un-confessed sin.
Josh. 12:1-4	The final score	Joshua and the Israelites defeated 31 kings.

The Division of the Promised Land	
Tribes East of the Jordan	Reuben, Gad, and half the tribe of Manasseh (Josh. 13)
Tribes West of the Jordan	All the rest of the tribes of Israel (Josh. 14-21)

Joshua's Farewell Addresses	
Josh. 22:5	Joshua tells the people to observe the commands given by Moses.
Josh. 23:14-16	Joshua encourages the people to continue following the LORD and warns of what would happen if they did not.
Josh. 24:14-15	Joshua challenges the people to choose to serve the LORD.

Josh. 21

The Book of Joshua records how the LORD fulfilled His promises (Josh. 21:43-45). He did what He said He would do—He created a great multitude of descendants from Abraham. He delivered His people from slavery in Egypt. He gave them a government like none the world had ever seen. And now He had given them rest and peace in the Promised Land. The end of the book of Joshua mentions that the Israelites served the LORD until Joshua and all the elders who outlived him passed away. The LORD had promised Israel great prosperity as long as they continued to live in the Promised Land and follow the statutes and commandments He had given them through Moses. But without Joshua's godly leadership, it remained to be seen if the next generation of Israelites would continue following the LORD.

Scene Eight:
Established in the Land of the Tribes (Judges, Ruth)

The book of Judges opens with a description of the Israelites' uncertainty following the death of Joshua. All of the tribes had taken *Judg. 1* their inheritance in the Promised Land, but they failed to completely drive out all of its previous inhabitants. There was also a lack of unity amongst the twelve tribes. Because of this, each Israelite tribe was separately hounded by their pagan neighbors.

The people's problems were the direct result of their disobedience. Moses had given the people three specific commands concerning what they were to do when they entered the Promised Land:

What Moses Said	What the Israelites Did
Utterly destroy the Canaanites; make no covenants; show no mercy (Deut. 7:2).	They put the Canaanites to forced labor but did not drive them out completely (Judg. 1:28).
Shun false gods; destroy their objects of pagan worship (Deut. (7:4-5).	They abandoned the LORD and went after other gods (Judg. 2:12).
Do not intermarry with pagan neighbors (Deut. 7:3).	They intermarried with their pagan neighbors and served their gods (Judg. 3:5-7).

There is a cycle that is repeated many times in the book of Judges. *Judg. 2* When the Israelites turned away from the LORD and began worshiping false gods, the LORD used pagan nations to discipline His people (Judg. 2:11-15). Their pursuit of sin led them into servitude to their foreign aggressors. Finding themselves suffering for their sin, the people cried out to God for mercy. The LORD heard their cry and raised up deliverers called judges. These judges were temporary, local leaders for times of crisis (Judg. 2:16-19). The LORD used them to deliver the people and redeem them from their enemies. The cycle is illustrated below:

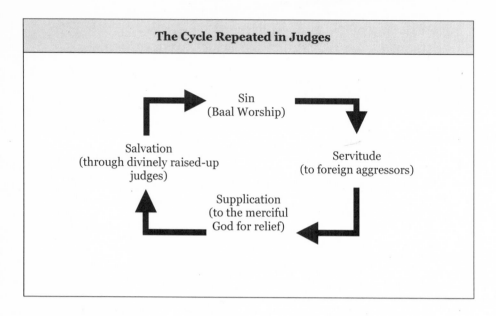

The Cycle Repeated in Judges

In all, Israel had thirteen judges:

The Judges of Israel		
Othniel	Defeated Cushan-rishathaim, king of Mesopotamia	Judg. 3:7-11
Ehud	Stabbed and killed Eglon, king of Moab	Judg. 3:12-30
Shamgar	Killed 600 Philistines with an ox goad	Judg. 3:31
Deborah	The only judge who was a woman, defeated Sisera, general of Canaan	Judg. 4-5
Gideon	Destroyed the altar of Baal, defeated the Midianites despite being outnumbered 450 to 1	Judg. 6-8

Tola	Judged Israel for 23 years	Judg. 10:1-2
Jair	Judged Israel for 22 years	Judg. 10:3-5
Jephthah	Defeated the Ammonites	Judg. 11:1-12:7
Ibzan	Judged Israel for seven years	Judg. 12:8-10
Elon	Judged Israel for ten years	Judg. 12:11-12
Abdon	Judged Israel for eight years	Judg. 12:13-15
Samson	Fought and killed many Philistines	Judg. 13-16
Samuel	The last judge, also a priest and prophet	1 & 2 Samuel

The book of Judges is characterized by increasing idolatry and immorality. The phrase that summarizes this period of Israelite history is often repeated in the book:

"In those days there was no king in Israel; every man did what was right in his own eyes." –Judg. 17:6; 18:1; 19:1; 21:25

This recurring phrase highlights Israel's developing need for a king. *Judg. 21* Although the people could have continued to live with the LORD as their only king, they rejected Him because of their sinfulness and self-will.

The story of Ruth is also set in the time of the judges (Ruth 1:1). Ruth was a Moabite Gentile who became part of the Israelite *Ruth 1* community because of her faithfulness to her mother-in-law Naomi (Ruth 1:16-18). Through a divinely guided series of events, she married an influential Israelite named Boaz. His role as her "kinsman redeemer" provides a beautiful illustration of the LORD's redeeming love for His people.

During this time in Israel, poverty sometimes forced families to sell their land, which was their God-given inheritance in the Promised Land. Having lost their husbands, widows such as Ruth and her mother-in-law Naomi would have experienced severe financial hardship, since at this time it was uncommon for women to work and earn wages like men. To provide for herself and Naomi, Ruth was following behind reapers in the wheat field, gathering the wheat they left behind, according to the provisions in the Mosaic Law (Lev. 19:9). Because of their poverty, Naomi was going to have to sell the parcel of land that was her family's inheritance. If she sold her field, Naomi would have little hope of ever regaining it. She was unable to redeem, or "buy back" the land for herself. Moses had commanded that the Year of Jubilee, when all land was returned to its original owner, was to be celebrated every 50 years. However, there is no record of it ever being observed. This left only one option for Naomi and Ruth: they needed a relative to purchase and redeem the field on their behalf. Boaz, a relative of Naomi's late husband, was the owner of the field where Ruth had been gathering grain. If he was willing, he could redeem the field for Ruth and Naomi, and also take Ruth to be his wife. Because of his love for Ruth, Boaz pursued this matter of redemption at the city gate (the "courthouse" of those days) without hesitation. It was not the field that motivated Boaz to become the kinsman redeemer; he purchased the field in order to marry Ruth.

The story of redemption in the book of Ruth is an accurate picture of God's overarching plan of redemption for the world. Throughout Scripture, He often refers to His people as his bride (both Israel and the Church, Is. 62:5; Rev. 21:9). Through His death on the Cross, He paid the price to redeem the world in order to gain His bride, the people He loves.

Ruth's story is more than just an illustration of God's redemption; she became an important part of the history of redemption. She and Boaz had a son named Obed, who became the father of Jesse, the father of King David. Ruth was the great grandmother of King David (Ruth 4:13-22), and part of the lineage of the Messiah Himself (Matt. 1:5).

At the close of the period of the Judges, the thing that the nation needed most was unity. The LORD had been faithfully delivering His people, but the 12 tribes were functioning as separate states, not a nation. Although a human king was not God's ideal, some form of government would be better than no government at all. What the people believed they needed was a political leader, a king.

Scene Nine:
Samuel the Prophet (1 & 2 Samuel)

Samuel was a child of prayer. His mother, Hannah, was unable to
have children (1 Sam 1:1-3). Her barrenness tormented her, and she   *1 Sam. 1*
cried out to the LORD to help her conceive a child, promising to
commit him to the LORD's service (1 Sam. 1:10-11). As He had done
for His chosen women before, the LORD granted Hannah's request
and gave her a son.

By establishing Samuel as His prophet, the LORD made a
channel through which to speak to His people. God spoke directly   *1 Sam. 3*
to Samuel. He was the last of the judges and the first of the
prophets:

> *"And Samuel grew, and the Lord was with him, and did let none
> of his words fall to the ground. And all Israel from Dan even to
> Beer-sheba knew that Samuel was established to be a prophet of
> the Lord. And the Lord appeared again in Shiloh: for the Lord
> revealed himself to Samuel in Shiloh by the word of the Lord." –
> 1 Sam. 3:19-21*

By establishing Samuel as a judge, the LORD began to reunify
His people. Samuel rebuilt the nation both politically and   *1 Sam. 7*
spiritually. He united Israel for the first time since Joshua died:

> *"Then Samuel took a stone, and set it between Mizpeh and Shen,
> and called the name of it Eben-ezer, saying, Hitherto hath the
> Lord helped us. So the Philistines were subdued, and they came
> no more into the coast of Israel: and the hand of the Lord was
> against the Philistines all the days of Samuel. And the cities
> which the Philistines had taken from Israel were restored to
> Israel, from Ekron even unto Gath; and the coasts thereof did
> Israel deliver out of the hands of the Philistines. And there was
> peace between Israel and the Amorites. And Samuel judged
> Israel all the days of his life. And he went from year to year in
> circuit to Beth-el, and Gilgal, and Mizpeh, and judged Israel in
> all those places. And his return was to Ramah; for there was his
> house; and there he judged Israel; and there he built an altar
> unto the Lord." –1 Sam. 7:12-17*

The LORD brought about a revival during Samuel's time as
prophet, priest and judge of Israel. The revival began with a praying
mother, a chastened people who sensed their need, and a faithful
prophet who followed the LORD whole-heartedly.

1 Sam. 8   Although the LORD did great things through Samuel, the people of Israel wanted more than a judge to lead them. They demanded a king:

> "Then all the elders of Israel gathered themselves together, and came to Samuel unto Ramah, and said unto him, Behold, thou art old, and thy sons walk not in thy ways: now make us a king to judge us like all the nations. But the thing displeased Samuel, when they said, Give us a king to judge us. And Samuel prayed unto the Lord. And the Lord said unto Samuel, Hearken unto the voice of the people in all that they say unto thee: for they have not rejected thee, but they have rejected me, that I should not reign over them. According to all the works which they have done since the day that I brought them up out of Egypt even unto this day, wherewith they have forsaken me, and served other gods, so do they also unto thee. Now therefore hearken unto their voice: howbeit yet protest solemnly unto them, and shew them the manner of the king that shall reign over them." -1 Sam. 8:4-9

The LORD gave the people what they asked for, but warned them of the consequences of appointing a king to rule over them. Even though He granted the people's misguided request, the LORD was working to build His great nation through which He would bring salvation to the world.

Scene Ten:
The Reign of Saul (1 Samuel 8-31)

The people of Israel demanded a king. The LORD foresaw this demand hundreds of years in advance. The LORD gave Moses His guidelines for Israel's kings, which Moses communicated in his address to all of the people. When Israel appointed a king, these were the rules they were to follow[6]:

God's Guidelines for Israel's Kings	
The king must be chosen by God.	Deut. 17:14-15
The king must be an Israelite.	Deut. 17:15
The king must not acquire many horses for himself, especially not from Egypt.	Deut. 17:16
The king must not acquire many wives for himself, lest his heart turn away from the LORD.	Deut. 17:17
The king must not acquire excessive silver and gold for himself.	Deut. 17:17
The king must write out a copy of the law and read it all the days of his life, and follow what it says.	Deut. 17:18-20

The problem with the people's request was that they wanted to be like the nations that surrounded them. The LORD had clearly instructed the people that they were to be distinct from other nations. They were to be known as a special people who had a special relationship with the living God. Instead of choosing to operate as a theocracy and be ruled by God, the people wanted a monarchy: a nation ruled by one human being. They choose human leadership over divine leadership, despite Samuel's warning of the costliness of having a king (1 Sam. 8).

---

[6] Compare with page 61.

The LORD gave the Israelites Saul as their leader (1 Sam. 9-12). Physically, he was everything they wanted; he was a tall, strong, handsome man who looked the part of a king. When Saul began to reign, he was humble and ruled well. In time, however, Saul's pride grew and grew until it turned him into a fool.

1 Sam. 9

Saul disobeyed the LORD by presumptuously offering sacrifices on the LORD's altar (1 Sam. 13), by failing to completely eradicate the Amalekites as the LORD had commanded (1 Sam. 15), and by seeking counsel from a witch (1 Sam. 28). Because Saul did not heed the LORD's word, the LORD rejected Saul from being king. David was anointed in Saul's place. As the LORD empowered David—helping him defeat Goliath and the Philistines—Saul became jealous and tried to kill David. Saul's carnal anger eventually led to the death of his own courageous, godly son Jonathan (1 Sam. 31). Saul's life is a tragic example of the devastating effects of pride.

1 Sam. 13

Scene Eleven:
The Reigns of David and Solomon (2 Samuel 1—1 Kings 10)

The first king of Israel was Saul, but he did not rule for God. What Israel needed was a theocratic monarchy: God ruling the nation through a man.

When Samuel reported the LORD's message to Saul, that he was rejected as king, he also said that the LORD had found "'a man after His own heart" who would do His will (1 Sam. 13:14). Samuel anointed David, a young shepherd from Bethlehem, as the next king. It would be 14 years before David became the king over all Israel, but his anointing was a monumental event:

1 Sam. 16

> *"Then Samuel took the horn of oil, and anointed him in the midst of his brethren; and the Spirit of the Lord came upon David from that day forward." —1 Sam. 16:13*

The first seven years following his anointing were important years of training for David. During these years, David learned to trust the LORD for deliverance. The LORD enabled him to defeat the bear, the lion, and the Philistine giant Goliath. He also learned to wait on the LORD and His timing. Despite David's faithful service as a warrior and musician, Saul became jealous of David and tried to kill him. For seven years, David's life was in constant danger. Although he had opportunities to kill Saul and take his throne, David refused to harm the king whom the LORD had anointed. This demonstrated his faith in the LORD; He had promised to make David king, and David trusted Him to do it.

After seven years of running from Saul, the king and his sons were killed in a battle with the Philistines (1 Sam. 31). Following Saul's death, David sought the LORD's will when he faced decisions (2 Sam. 2:1; 5:22-23). David desired to listen to the LORD and follow His will. As a result, the LORD directed David's steps to the throne. For the first seven years after Saul's death, David ruled over the region of Judah only, while the rest of Israel was largely controlled by the Philistines. Through a series of divinely-directed battles, all Israel became united under David's theocratic leadership (2 Sam. 1:1-5). David moved the tabernacle and the Ark of the Covenant from Gibeah (Saul's capital) to Jerusalem. Moses had commanded the people to sacrifice together at the tabernacle's permanent location, a place which the LORD Himself would choose. Once the tabernacle settled in Jerusalem, God's chosen

1 Sam. 31

2 Sam. 1

place, the nation had a permanent place to come together and worship the LORD as His unified people.

2 Sam. 7

Having built the nation He had promised to build, the LORD renewed His promise of redemption to David. David wanted to build a permanent temple to replace the moveable tabernacle that had been used since the days of Moses. The LORD's reply to David was that instead of David building a house for the LORD, the LORD would build David's house (i.e. his dynasty). He promised David a dynasty, an everlasting throne, and an everlasting kingdom. God's reign over the earth would come through David's descendants. David knew how important this promise was, and how it fit within the LORD's plan of redemption and His promises to David's ancestors (2 Sam. 7:23-25; 1 Chron. 17). David thanked God for giving him this promise, praised God for all He had done in the past, and prayed for God to fulfill His promise in the future. The Messianic and redemptive implications of the LORD's promise to David are clear, and the fulfillment of this promise was finally confirmed when the angel Gabriel appeared to Mary, the mother of Jesus, and spoke these words to her:

> *"And behold, thou shalt conceive in thy womb, and bring forth a son, and shalt call his name JESUS. He shall be great, and shall be called the Son of the Highest: and the Lord God shall give unto him the throne of his father David: and he shall reign over the house of Jacob for ever; and of his kingdom there shall be no end." -Luke 1:31-33*

Although many of the kings in David's lineage turned away from following the LORD and forfeited their personal share in His promise, they transmitted the promise to their descendants, and the Word of God was fulfilled; David's lineage remained unbroken all the way to the coming of the Messiah, whose kingdom is everlasting.

2 Sam. 12

David was not perfect in every respect. His adultery with Bathsheba and his consequent murder of her husband Uriah amounted to a moral failure of horrifying seriousness (2 Sam. 11). But unlike Saul, whose repentance was neither genuine nor lasting (1 Sam. 15:24-31) David truly humbled himself and confessed his sin completely, and turned back to God with his whole heart (2 Sam. 12:13-14; 2 Cor. 7:10). David's godly grief over his sin can be seen and felt by reading Psalms 32 and 51, his psalms of repentance. David's fellowship with the LORD was restored, but there were irrevocable consequences for his sin. The child

Bathsheba conceived by David died. Nevertheless, the LORD did not allow the story to end in tragedy.

Later, after the death of their first child, Bathsheba gave birth to a son, whom they named Solomon. It was Solomon who received the promise of the LORD, who said that He would be a father to him and assured him that he was the one to build a house (i.e. the temple) for the LORD's name to dwell in Jerusalem.

David publicly appointed Solomon as his successor, making an oath to his wife Bathsheba: *1 Ki. 1*

> *"Then king David answered and said, 'Call me Bath-sheba'. And she came into the king's presence, and stood before the king. And the king sware, and said, 'As the Lord liveth, that hath redeemed my soul out of all distress, even as I sware unto thee by the Lord God of Israel, saying, Assuredly Solomon thy son shall reign after me, and he shall sit upon my throne in my stead; even so will I certainly do this day.' Then Bath-sheba bowed with her face to the earth, and did reverence to the king, and said, 'Let my lord king David live for ever.'" -1 Kings 1:28-31*

As David approached his death, he urged his son to follow the LORD and to keep His commandments as they were written in the Law of Moses. And Solomon loved the LORD (1 Kings 3:3).   *1 Ki. 3*

The LORD appeared to Solomon at the beginning of his reign, asking him what He should give him. Solomon's answer was marked by thankfulness and a humble recognition of his need for the LORD's wisdom in his new role as the king over God's people:

> *"Thou hast shewed unto thy servant David my father great mercy, according as he walked before thee in truth, and in righteousness, and in uprightness of heart with thee; and thou hast kept for him this great kindness, that thou hast given him a son to sit on his throne, as it is this day. And now, O Lord my God, thou hast made thy servant king instead of David my father: and I am but a little child: I know not how to go out or come in. And thy servant is in the midst of thy people which thou hast chosen, a great people, that cannot be numbered nor counted for multitude. Give therefore thy servant an understanding heart to judge thy people, that I may discern between good and bad: for who is able to judge this thy so great a people?" -1 Kings 3:6-9*

Citing the LORD's promise to David, Solomon planned to build a temple for the LORD (1 Kings 5:4-5). He knew that he was chosen   *1 Ki. 5* to complete this project, so he began to build a glorious temple using the most precious building materials he could acquire.

1 Ki. 8   The LORD filled the temple with His glory just as He had filled the tabernacle in Moses' day. Since God is an omnipresent, infinite Spirit, no human building could ever contain His totality. But by filling the temple with his glory, the LORD was visibly manifesting his presence at the center of His nation (1 Kings 8:10-13; cf. 1 Kings 8:27, Ps. 139, Acts 7:47-50).

1 Ki. 10   Because Solomon's request for wisdom pleased the LORD, He also gave him unsurpassed riches and honor. Even the eminent Queen of Sheba came to visit Solomon because of his fame. After seeing the blessings the LORD had poured out on Solomon and his kingdom, she reported that even the magnificent stories she had heard about him were insufficient to describe his greatness (1 Kings 10:6-9). Solomon excelled all the kings of the earth (1 Kings 10:23-25).

Act One ends on a glorious note: Israel is a theocratic nation where God is ruling His people. Their king, who loved the LORD, built Him a house; and the LORD filled the house with the glory of His presence.

God Speaks: The Davidic Covenant and the Poetic Books
(Job; Psalms; Proverbs; Ecclesiastes; Song of Songs)

God spoke to David at a high point in Israel's theocracy, promising that the Messiah would come through David's line of descendants (2 Sam. 7; 1 Chron. 17). During this era, God also spoke *through* David and others who contributed to the Poetic Books.

The Need: The nation appeared to have everything they needed at this point: they had a king who was ruling for God and they had the grace of God bringing them all of the blessings they had been promised. The one need David saw was the need to build a permanent house for God. This was a need that the LORD chose Solomon to satisfy. Through the Poetic Books, the LORD addressed the need for His truth to be within His people's hearts, not only in the external, ritual form of their worship.

The Content: The books in this section are all in poetic form. They reflect the inner experiences of God's people in five different aspects of life:

- *Job – The heart of a man of God trusting God in spite of suffering*
- *Psalms – The heart of the people of God in various circumstances*
- *Proverbs – The heart of the people of God as they wisely face the practical affairs of life*
- *Ecclesiastes – The heart of a man of God as he seeks meaning apart from God*
- *Song of Solomon – The heart of a man and woman of God in marriage*

The Method: God's message in these books is in the form of testimony. Although it seems like these are only man's words being spoken to God, God is actually speaking in the experiences of His people, who have in their hearts what God wants to communicate. Look up the following passages of Scripture to see how David's words were also God's Word: Acts 1:16; 4:25; Heb. 4:6-7.

The Response Required: We can take these words and say or sing them back to God. We can make these our very own words. For example, we can pray through a Psalm. Why not use the Psalms for our own times of prayer and praise?

ACT TWO

God scatters and
restores
the nation.

1 Kings 11 – 2 Chronicles 36
Ezra, Nehemiah, and Esther

Scene One:
The Decline and Fall of Solomon (1 Kings 11)

Israel reached its political zenith under Solomon. His kingdom extended from the Euphrates River in the north to the border of Egypt in the south. In this the LORD's promises to Abraham and Moses were fulfilled:

> *"In the same day the LORD made a covenant with Abram, saying, Unto thy seed have I given this land, from the river of Egypt unto the great river, the river Euphrates." –Gen. 15:18*

> *"Every place whereon the soles of your feet shall tread shall be yours: from the wilderness and Lebanon, from the river, the river Euphrates, even unto the uttermost sea shall your coast be." –Deut. 11:24*

> *"And Solomon reigned over all kingdoms from the river unto the land of the Philistines, and unto the border of Egypt: they brought presents, and served Solomon all the days of his life." –1 Kin. 4:21*

Through Samuel, the LORD had warned Israel of the dangers of having a king (1 Sam. 8:10-22). Just as Samuel had warned, Solomon's glory came at a heavy cost to his people. He drafted workers who were subjected to forced labor on his building projects (1 Kings 5:13-16). Another indication of a problem with Solomon was the fact that he spent more time constructing his own house than he did the house of God (1 Kin. 6:37—7:1).

In Deuteronomy 17:14-20, the LORD had given specific guidelines for Israel's kings to follow (see p. 47). By the end of his reign, Solomon had violated these specific commands, which his father had instructed him to follow: (1) he acquired excessive amounts of silver and gold (1 Kin. 10:14-25, 27); (2) he acquired many horses and chariots from Egypt (1 Kin. 10:26-29); he acquired many foreign wives who turned his heart away from the LORD (1 Kin. 11:1-8)[7].

After Solomon constructed the temple in Jerusalem, the LORD appeared to Him again, as He had done at the beginning of Solomon's reign. This time the LORD promised Solomon that His Name would dwell in Jerusalem forever. The LORD said:

---

[7] Compare with page 51.

"I have hallowed this house, which thou hast built, to put my name there for ever; and mine eyes and mine heart shall be there perpetually." –1 Kin.9:3

As with the LORD's other promises, Solomon's personal experience of the blessing the LORD promised was conditioned on his response to God's word. If he followed the LORD, he would continue to be blessed according to the LORD's promise. But if he turned away from the LORD, the nation would suffer great loss:

"But if ye shall at all turn from following me, ye or your children, and will not keep my commandments and my statutes which I have set before you, but go and serve other gods, and worship them: Then will I cut off Israel out of the land which I have given them; and this house, which I have hallowed for my name, will I cast out of my sight; and Israel shall be a proverb and a byword among all people: And at this house, which is high, every one that passeth by it shall be astonished, and shall hiss; and they shall say, Why hath the LORD done thus unto this land, and to this house? And they shall answer, Because they forsook the LORD their God, who brought forth their fathers out of the land of Egypt, and have taken hold upon other gods, and have worshipped them, and served them: therefore hath the LORD brought upon them all this evil." –1 Kin.9:6-9

1 Ki. 11   The LORD became angry with Solomon because of his blatant disregard for God's command against marrying pagan women (1 Kin. 11:9). Apparently, Solomon's love for foreign princesses eclipsed his love for the LORD (cf. 1 Kin. 3:3; 11:1-2). These women enticed Solomon to turn away from the true God and follow their pagan abominations. As he had sworn to David and to Solomon himself, the LORD chastened Solomon by raising up adversaries against him (2 Sam. 7:14; 1 Kin. 11:9-43). Despite His chastening, the LORD did not revoke His promise to provide an heir for David. God's promise was passed on, but Solomon's glorious kingdom now warranted God's judgment. In spite of all God had done for him, Solomon's spiritual life and his love for God had declined so far that he had completely lost his fellowship with His LORD, whom he once loved.

The three kings of Israel's united monarchy were Saul, David and Solomon. The united monarchy lasted for 120 years. Saul spent forty years establishing the nation, David spent forty years expanding the nation, and Solomon spent forty years glorifying the nation.

Scene Two:
The Nation is Divided in 931 B.C. (1 Kings 12)

Solomon contributed to Israel materially, but not spiritually. He was weak with regard to the temptations of luxurious living: sex, money, and glory (cf. Deut. 17:14f). God had spoken beforehand about what would happen if Solomon turned away from him (1 Sam. 7; 1 Kings 9:6-7). God chastened Solomon by raising up opposition from surrounding nations, but the main threat was from within his kingdom.

In 1 Kings 11, the LORD told Solomon that He was going to do something about the nation's moral and spiritual deterioration. He used an able man named Jeroboam to divide the nation. Jeroboam opposed Solomon's heavy labor requirements which he imposed on the people of Israel. Through the prophet Ahijah, the LORD promised Jeroboam that he would give him ten tribes of Israel. The LORD also informed Solomon of what He was going to do. Upon hearing the news, Solomon tried to kill Jeroboam, who fled to Egypt for safety.

After Solomon's death, the people summoned Jeroboam who came back from Egypt to represent the people's request for Solomon's son Reheboam to lighten the hard service requirements that Solomon had imposed. The older counselors advised Reheboam: *1 Ki. 12*

> *"If thou wilt be a servant unto this people this day, and wilt serve them, and answer them, and speak good words to them, then they will be thy servants for ever." –1 Kin.12:7*

Reheboam spurned the advice of the elders and followed the counsel of the young men whom he had grown up with. Instead of lightening the people's work load, he tried to make a display of ruthless power, promising to increase their labor and discipline them more harshly than his father had. This was more than Jeroboam and the people could bear, and Reheboam's attempt to assert his power backfired; ten tribes of Israel seceded from the nation and made Jeroboam their king. This left Reheboam ruling only over Jerusalem and its surrounding area of Judah. In 931 B.C., the nation was divided into two: Israel and Judah.

A civil war seemed unavoidable after Jeroboam and the ten tribes of Israel killed Rehoboam's taskmaster Adoram when he was sent to reclaim his laborers from Israel. But the LORD intervened to save His people from killing each other in what surely would have been a horrific and devastating civil war. Through Shemaiah, a man of God, the LORD declared His will to Reheboam and the people of Judah:

> *"Thus saith the LORD, Ye shall not go up, nor fight against your brethren the children of Israel: return every man to his house; for this thing is from me. They hearkened therefore to the word of the LORD, and returned to depart, according to the word of the LORD." –1 Kin.12:24*

The LORD used Reheboam's foolishness and the people's distress over forced labor to bring about a turn of events that accomplished His purposes for the people. Even the heart-wrenching judgment of His nation fit within God's plan to provide redemption for the world.

It is natural to wonder why the Messiah did not arrive during Solomon's reign. At that time, the LORD had fulfilled every aspect of His promises to Noah, Abraham and David. The only part missing was for the Redeemer to actually appear and bring the salvation that was promised for all nations. Why did the world have to wait for the Messiah? Surely, Solomon's slide into sin had a lot to do with it, but the main reason seems to be given by Paul in Galatians 4:4: the "fullness of time" had not yet arrived.

Scene Three:
The Ten Northern Tribes of Israel are Removed and Scattered by Assyria in 722 B.C. (1 Kings 13—2 Kings 17)

The biblical account of Jeroboam illustrates the fairness and equity of God's dealings with His people. Even though Jeroboam was used in God's plan to divide the nation, he was not excused from his own moral accountability to God. He feared that if the ten northern tribes continued to worship at the temple in Jerusalem, their loyalty would turn back to Reheboam. Jeroboam set up two golden calves to represent new centers of worship at Dan and Bethel, and set up a system of religion which he had "devised of his own heart" (1 Kin. 12:33). This was an act of direct disobedience to God's commands. Because of Jeroboam's sin of false worship, the LORD declared that his dynasty was doomed and that He eventually would uproot Israel and scatter them from their land (1 Kin. 14:14-16).

1 Ki. 13

1 Ki. 14

"The sins of Jeroboam" became the recurring theme of the northern kingdom of Israel. Of the 19 kings who ruled the northern kingdom, not a single one was considered "good" by God. All of them rejected the true worship of the LORD and followed either the substitute worship system at the golden calf centers or the cult of Baal.

Israel began paying tribute to Tiglath-pilesar III (as Assyria's slaves) around 745 B.C. When that king died, Israel rebelled against Assyria. This forced the Assyrians, under Shalmaneser V followed by Sargon II, to take action by coming and decimating Israel. The Israelites were dragged out of the Promised Land in 722 B.C., and the pagan multitudes (later called "Samaritans") were brought in.

A thorough comparison between Deuteronomy 28 and 2 Kings 17 reveals that the LORD accurately forewarned His people throughout their entire history of what would happen if they turned away from Him, their Redeemer. The reason for Israel's judgment is summarized in 2 Kings 17:

2 Ki. 17

> "For so it was, that the children of Israel had sinned against the LORD their God, which had brought them up out of the land of Egypt, from under the hand of Pharaoh king of Egypt, and had feared other gods, and walked in the statutes of the heathen, whom the LORD cast out from before the children of Israel, and of the kings of Israel, which they had made." –2 Kin. 17:7-8

Two hundred years after the LORD told Jeroboam it would happen, the northern kingdom was dragged into captivity in Assyria, because they had forsaken their LORD in favor of the false gods of their surrounding nations.

Scene Four:
The Two Southern Tribes of Judah are Removed and Scattered by the Babylonians in 586 B.C. (2 Kings 17—2 Chronicles 36)

According to 2 Kings 17:19, Judah walked in Israel's footsteps and followed the same wicked customs and false worship that Israel introduced. God's chosen people were engaging in the same idolatry and morally reprehensible acts as the previous inhabitants of the Promised Land, whom the LORD had judged by giving their land to the Israelites. In their conquest of the land of Canaan, the Israelites did not obey the LORD's command to completely eliminate the population of these wicked nations from the Promised Land. Because of this failure, many Canaanites lived as neighbors to the Israelites and influenced them religiously and morally. According to Leviticus 20, the shameful and disgusting acts of the Canaanites included infant sacrifice to the false god Molech, adultery, incest, homosexuality and sexual relations with animals. These practices were the reason why, after 400 years, the LORD finally judged the Canaanites through Israel's conquest of the Promised Land. The LORD said:

> "And ye shall not walk in the manners of the nation, which I cast out before you: for they committed all these things, and therefore I abhorred them. But I have said unto you, Ye shall inherit their land, and I will give it unto you to possess it, a land that floweth with milk and honey: I am the LORD your God, which have separated you from other people. Ye shall therefore put difference between clean beasts and unclean, and between unclean fowls and clean: and ye shall not make your souls abominable by beast, or by fowl, or by any manner of living thing that creepeth on the ground, which I have separated from you as unclean. And ye shall be holy unto me: for I the LORD am holy, and have severed you from other people, that ye should be mine." –Lev. 20:23-26

Both the northern kingdom of Israel and the southern kingdom of Judah violated the LORD's command to be holy witnesses to the nations of the world. They were chosen to be holy as God is holy, now they had become corrupted like their wicked neighbors. During the reign of Judah's most wicked king, Manasseh, the LORD revealed the judgment that was coming upon Judah:

2 Ki. 21

> "And the LORD spake by his servants the prophets, saying, Because Manasseh king of Judah hath done these abominations, and hath done wickedly above all that the Amorites did, which

were before him, and hath made Judah also to sin with his idols: Therefore thus saith the LORD God of Israel, Behold, I am bringing such evil upon Jerusalem and Judah, that whosoever heareth of it, both his ears shall tingle. And I will stretch over Jerusalem the line of Samaria, and the plummet of the house of Ahab: and I will wipe Jerusalem as a man wipeth a dish, wiping it, and turning it upside down. And I will forsake the remnant of mine inheritance, and deliver them into the hand of their enemies; and they shall become a prey and a spoil to all their enemies; Because they have done that which was evil in my sight, and have provoked me to anger, since the day their fathers came forth out of Egypt, even unto this day." –2 Kin. 21:10-15

2 Chr. 33   Manasseh personally tasted this judgment when the LORD allowed him to be captured by the Assyrians and brutally exported to Babylon. Surprisingly, this notoriously wicked king, repented and humbled himself before the LORD (2 Chron. 33:10-20). Unfortunately, the people of Judah did not follow Manasseh's repentance after his return from Babylon, and their day of judgment was drawing closer than ever.

2 Chr. 36   During their apostasy, the LORD faithfully and persistently called His people to turn back to Him, but they refused to listen:

"And the LORD God of their fathers sent to them by his messengers, rising up betimes, and sending; because he had compassion on his people, and on his dwelling place: but they mocked the messengers of God, and despised his words, and misused his prophets, until the wrath of the LORD arose against his people, till there was no remedy." –2 Chron. 36:15-16

In three waves of attack (605, 597 and 586 B.C.), the Babylonians destroyed Jerusalem and took the people captive (2 Chron. 36:17-21). Jeremiah, who prophesied before, during and after the Babylonian invasion, gave the LORD's perspective on the Babylonian exile:

"And hast brought forth thy people Israel out of the land of Egypt with signs, and with wonders, and with a strong hand, and with a stretched out arm, and with great terror; And hast given them this land, which thou didst swear to their fathers to give them, a land flowing with milk and honey; And they came in, and possessed it; but they obeyed not thy voice, neither walked in thy law; they have done nothing of all that thou commandedst them to do: therefore thou hast caused all this evil to come upon them."
–Jer. 32:21-23

The LORD used Babylon against His people, but He did so for their ultimate good. They had resisted the LORD so much that judgment and exile was the only thing that could create a change. Since Israel's sin was idolatry, the LORD placed them in Babylon, the center of idol worship. The LORD used Babylon to cure His people of idolatry. As they lived in captivity in a foreign land, the people began to long for the fellowship they once had with the LORD in Jerusalem, the place the LORD had chosen (Deut. 12:5-26; 2 Chron. 6:6). Psalm 137 captures their longing:

> *"By the rivers of Babylon, there we sat down, yea, we wept, when we remembered Zion. We hanged our harps upon the willows in the midst thereof. For there they that carried us away captive required of us a song; and they that wasted us required of us mirth, saying, Sing us one of the songs of Zion. How shall we sing the LORD'S song in a strange land? If I forget thee, O Jerusalem, let my right hand forget her cunning. If I do not remember thee, let my tongue cleave to the roof of my mouth; if I prefer not Jerusalem above my chief joy." –Psa. 137:1-6*

As God's chosen people found themselves cut off from the Promised Land because of their sin, it looked as if God's instrument of redemption had been destroyed. But the LORD was not without an answer even in this disaster. He used this stroke of judgment to prepare the world for the coming of the Messiah. During the exile, prophets like Ezekiel and Daniel were the LORD's vessels for revealing His will to His people.

Perspectives of Kings and Chronicles	
1 & 2 Kings	**1 & 2 Chronicles**
Basically a *political* viewpoint	Basically a *spiritual* viewpoint
Written by a prophet	Written by a priest
Delivers a message of judgment	Delivers a message of hope
Recurring theme is human failure	Recurring theme is God's faithfulness

Summary of the Kings of Israel and Judah	
Israel (Northern Kingdom)	**Judah (Southern Kingdom)**
9 dynasties	1 dynasty (Davidic)
19 kings (none "good")	19 kings (8 "good")
No revivals	4 great revivals
Dispersion (Assyria)	Exile (Babylon)

Scene Five:
The People Return to Jerusalem and Rebuild the Temple (Ezra)

Nebuchadnezzar and the Babylonians (along with the Medes) had *Ez. 1* conquered Assyria around 610 B.C. At that time, the descendants of the captives from the northern kingdom of Israel were under Assyria's rule, and many of them were living in Babylon, Assyria's southern province. Consequently, when Nebuchadnezzar overthrew Judah, the captives from both Israel and Judah were brought together under the same foreign ruler. Almost 1,000 years after their exodus from Egypt, God's people found themselves in the same circumstance again. They were a common people living under a foreign power.

Cyrus' Persian forces conquered Babylon in 539 B.C. In the first year of Cyrus' reign, he issued a proclamation throughout his kingdom that God had told him to rebuild the temple in Jerusalem (Ez. 1:1-4). He commanded that the Israelites return to Jerusalem and rebuild the house of the LORD. Their neighbors in Babylon were to support them with gifts of silver and gold, livestock, and other offerings.

Through the prophet Isaiah, the LORD predicted Cyrus' decree, even calling the Persian king by name before he was born:

"That saith of Cyrus, He is my shepherd, and shall perform all my pleasure: even saying to Jerusalem, Thou shalt be built; and to the temple, Thy foundation shall be laid. Thus saith the LORD to his anointed, to Cyrus, whose right hand I have holden, to subdue nations before him; and I will loose the loins of kings, to open before him the two leaved gates; and the gates shall not be shut." –Is. 44:28, 45:1

Jeremiah, a prophet whose life ended before Cyrus ruled Babylon, prophesied:

"For thus saith the LORD, That after seventy years be accomplished at Babylon I will visit you, and perform my good word toward you, in causing you to return to this place. For I know the thoughts that I think toward you, saith the LORD, thoughts of peace, and not of evil, to give you an expected end." –Jer. 29:10-11

Zerubbabel, along with Joshua the high priest, was the leader
of the first wave of returners in 538 B.C. 50,000 Israelites traversed
700 miles of trackless desert to get back to the place where they
could worship the LORD at His temple again. Right away, they
rebuilt the altar, celebrated the Feast of Tabernacles, and began
rebuilding the temple. The Scriptures praise these people for doing
God's will.

Because of opposition from the Samaritans and other non-
Jewish inhabitants of Judah, no work was done on the temple for
about ten years. Instead of working on the temple, the people
retreated from the opposition and worked on their own houses.
Then Haggai began to prophesy, around 520 B.C., with his friend
and fellow prophet Zechariah. These two prophets challenged and
encouraged the people to complete the rebuilding of the temple.

In Haggai's prophecy, Zerubbabel is mentioned as a symbol of
the coming Messiah (signet rings leave an impression or copy, like
the tabernacle, Hag. 2). In Zechariah's vision, the high priest
Joshua is symbolically crowned to prefigure the Messiah (Zech. 6).
Haggai and Zechariah complemented each other's ministries,
encouraging the people to do the work God had called them to:

> *"Yet now be strong, O Zerubbabel, saith the LORD; and be
> strong, O Joshua, son of Josedech, the high priest; and be strong,
> all ye people of the land, saith the LORD, and work: for I am
> with you, saith the LORD of hosts: According to the word that I
> covenanted with you when ye came out of Egypt, so my spirit
> remaineth among you: fear ye not." –Hag. 2:4-5*

> *"Then he answered and spake unto me, saying, This is the word
> of the LORD unto Zerubbabel, saying, Not by might, nor by
> power, but by my spirit, saith the LORD of hosts. Who art thou,
> O great mountain? before Zerubbabel thou shalt become a plain:
> and he shall bring forth the headstone thereof with shoutings,
> crying, Grace, grace unto it." –Zech. 4:6-7*

They taught the people how to understand their present, partial
restoration as a reason to believe in God's Promise for the future
Messianic kingdom. God said he would bring them back from
captivity, and He did it. Therefore, the people should trust Him to
keep His Promise. As God promised, the temple was completed
under Zerubbabel, the same leader who started the work (Zech.
4:9), around 515 B.C.

When the foundation was laid for the temple, it was greeted
with mixed reactions from the people:

Ez. 2

Ez. 3

"And they sang together by course in praising and giving thanks unto the LORD; because he is good, for his mercy endureth for ever toward Israel. And all the people shouted with a great shout, when they praised the LORD, because the foundation of the house of the LORD was laid. But many of the priests and Levites and chief of the fathers, who were ancient men, that had seen the first house, when the foundation of this house was laid before their eyes, wept with a loud voice; and many shouted aloud for joy: So that the people could not discern the noise of the shout of joy from the noise of the weeping of the people: for the people shouted with a loud shout, and the noise was heard afar off." —Ez. 3:11-13

"Who is left among you that saw this house in her first glory? And how do ye see it now? is it not in your eyes in comparison of it as nothing." —Hag. 2:3

In 458 B.C., Ezra led the second of three waves of exiles back to Judah (Ez. 7). It had been over 50 years since the temple was reconstructed, and Ezra wanted to evaluate the spiritual condition of the nation. He was concerned with Israel's sacred heritage and holy writings. As Ezra and the returning exiles approached Jerusalem, Ezra proclaimed a fast and gathered gifts for an offering at the restored temple. Ezra was also an excellent expositor and communicator of the written Word of God (Ez. 7:10; Neh. 8:4-8). He faithfully studied it, practiced it, and explained it to others. As he called the people back to God's law (probably the Book of the Law written by Moses referenced in Deut. 31:24-26), they responded to the conviction of God's truth by repenting from all of their deviant practices.

Ez. 7

By the time Ezra arrived, he found that the people of Judah had already fallen into sin by intermarrying with their pagan neighbors. The improper marriages between the Israelites and pagan women were probably not legal marriages. The problem was not the ethnicity of the women but their religious beliefs and practices, which led the Israelites into idolatry. In the same way as Solomon had fallen, the people were now repeating the sin that had caused their captivity. Ezra led the people to confess their sin and dissolve their improper marriages. He preached God's Word and the people repented. He also reorganized the priesthood to provide spiritual leadership for the people (Ez. 10).

Ez. 10

The book of Ezra shows God's power and faithfulness to provide redemption through His chosen people, using even pagan kings to fulfill His redemptive purposes, just as He had promised.

Scene Six:
The Wall of Jerusalem is Rebuilt (Nehemiah)

Nehemiah led the third wave of exiles back to Judah, returning around 445 B.C. Despite heavy opposition and treachery, *Neh. 1* Nehemiah unified and inspired the people to rebuild the walls of Jerusalem in 52 days. He chose wise defensive measures and trusted the LORD to protect him and the people. He did what the LORD called him to do with the joy of the LORD as his strength (Neh. 8:10). When the people began to fall into sin, Nehemiah had *Neh. 8* Ezra read to them from the Book of the Law, which led to the people's repentance. The people cleansed the temple, made their hearts right with God, offered their tithes, reinstituted the Sabbath, and removed the pagan women from the community of Israel.

Only a portion of the exiles returned to the Promised Land. The rest were still scattered throughout the 127 provinces of Persia. The Jews that did not return established small assemblies in Persia called synagogues where the faithful could receive teaching and worship the LORD. The nation as a whole did not return to the Promised Land, and even those who had returned were still under foreign rule.

Another disappointment was that the presence of God never visibly filled the second temple as it had filled the Tabernacle (Ex. 40:34-35) and Solomon's temple (1 Kin. 8:10-11). The Ark of the Covenant, the most important symbol of God's abiding presence among His people, was missing from the rebuilt temple. But the Messianic lineage was restored to the land, and that was the most important result of the return from exile.

"Chapter 9" Prayers of Confession	
Ezra 9	The Israelites confess and repent of improper marriages.
Nehemiah 9	The Israelites confess their wickedness.
Daniel 9	Daniel prays and confesses his people's guilt.

Scene Seven:
The LORD Protects His People in Exile (Esther)

Esth. 1

The book of Esther fits between chapters 6 and 7 of Ezra. Esther was written from the perspective of the Jews who chose not to return to Judah with Zerubbabel, Ezra, or Nehemiah. It would have been hard for them to leave Persia, but it would have pleased God. They could have taken an active part in redemptive history, but chose to remain in exile. Only a relatively small remnant of Jews really cared enough about the LORD and His purposes to make the journey back to Jerusalem.

The story of Esther demonstrates God's faithfulness to the people He loves and to His covenant. It also shows how He can do His will despite powerful rulers, evil schemes and less-than-perfect servants. Although the book of Esther never mentions God's name, He was clearly orchestrating all of its events.

Esth. 3

Since the promised Messiah would come from Judah, Esther's relationship to the history of redemption is not direct. But because Judah was under the rule of Persia, the Jews in Jerusalem would have been killed along with the Jews in Babylon when the Persian ruler Ahasueras issued his decree to exterminate all of the Jews.

Esth. 8

The progress of redemption was taking place in Judah, but the LORD exercised His amazing sovereign power over human government to protect His people and guarantee that His plan of redemption would continue through the Jews. Ultimately, the LORD's protection of the Jews through Esther defeated Satan's attempt to thwart God's redemptive plan.

After the close of Nehemiah, 400 years of silence followed. The books of Job through Malachi retrace and amplify the history that had already been described in the historical books. These poetic and prophetic books contain what God said throughout those years.

God Speaks: The Prophetic Books
(Isaiah—Malachi)

In the absence of a king who ruled for God, the people strayed from their covenant with God. During this time, the prophets were called by God to be His faithful spokespersons. They spoke to the people of Israel, forth-telling God's messages and also foretelling future events in His redemptive program.

The Need: The chosen people needed God to speak at this time. They had broken the moral law and corrupted the ceremonial law (see Isa. 1:2). The need was to restore the broken relationship.

The Content: What went wrong? Through the prophets, God spoke about the problems of the broken relationship: its cause, its consequences, and its solution. He makes it clear He was not the cause (see Micah 6:3). Look up the following passages to fully grasp the need: Jeremiah 13:11; Hosea 3:1; Ezekiel 16:8-22. God had entered into a wonderful relationship with Israel and they had broken it. They turned to idols. In some of the prophetic writings, the LORD spoke of Israel as his wife. Marital problems are one thing, but if the wife turns to the husband and says she has fallen in love with another, that is something much more serious. Hosea illustrates this through his experience.

The Method: The Lord was now speaking primarily through His prophets (Deuteronomy 18:15-22). Each of the prophets had to have a sovereign calling from God and God-given abilities. Some prophets only spoke their messages (two of which were Elijah and Elisha), while others also wrote down their messages for future generations. The prophetic books were written starting at about 90 years after the division of the Northern and Southern kingdoms (Israel and Judah). Some prophets ministered before the exile of Israel (to Assyria in 722 B.C.) and Judah (to Babylon in 596 B.C.): Obadiah and Joel (9th century B.C.); Amos, Hosea, Jonah, Micah, and Isaiah (8th century B.C.). Some prophesied during the exile: Nahum, Zephaniah, Habakkuk, and Jeremiah (7th century B.C.); Ezekiel and Daniel (6th century B.C.). And others spoke for the LORD after the exile was over: Haggai and Zechariah (6th century B.C.); Malachi (5th century B.C.). The LORD was faithful to speak to His people before, during, and after their judgment came.

The Response Required: The proper response was threefold: (1) admit the failure (confession), (2) turn back to the faithful, loving God (repentance), and (3) go on walking with Him in faith and obedience.

ACT THREE

God comes to the
nation and provides
redemption.

The Gospels

Scene One:
Messiah Comes to Provide Redemption (Matthew—John)

Matthew began his Gospel with a review of the history of redemption preceding the coming of the Messiah:

> i) God builds a nation: *"So all the generations from Abraham to David were fourteen generations..."*
> ii) God judges the nation: *"...and from David until the captivity in Babylon were fourteen generations..."*
> iii) God restores the nation: *"...and from the Babylon deportation to Christ were fourteen generations." –Matt. 1:17*

The four Gospels present the ultimate reason for the nation of Israel: through this nation the LORD sent His Messiah who provided salvation for the world (John 4:22).

The Gospels are faithful and inspired records of the work and words of Jesus Christ. Luke described his Gospel as his account "of all that Jesus began both to *do* and to *teach*" (Acts 1:1). Here was God on earth; fully God and fully man. He was the Redeemer, the Messiah the world awaited. He broke into human history to save us from our sins and capture our hearts with words of hope. Jesus—His incarnation, life, sacrifice, and resurrection—is the fulcrum of human history. The entire Old Testament was leading up to this point.

Comparison of the Gospels and Acts	
Matthew	Jesus Christ is the King of the Jews (2:2)
Mark	Jesus Christ is the Servant of the LORD (10:45)
Luke	Jesus Christ is the Son of Man (Luke 19:10)
John	Jesus Christ is the Son of God (1:1)
Acts	Jesus Christ is the Ascended Lord of All (1:10)

For 400 hundred years after Nehemiah, the stage was being set for the coming of the Messiah. The timing of His coming had to be perfect. Reflecting on the timing of Christ's coming, Paul wrote in his letter to the Galatians:

> *"But when the fullness of the time was come, God sent forth his Son, made of a woman, made under the law, to redeem them that were under the law, that we might receive the adoption of sons."* –Gal. 4:4-5

The "fullness of time" was characterized by the following six features:

1. Worldwide centralization: Rome ruled what was then the known civilized world.

2. Worldwide cultural oneness: the Roman Empire combined the best of the existing cultures into one.

3. Worldwide trade and communication: the Greek language was the language used internationally. There was freedom to trade in every area.

4. Worldwide peace: the presence of the Roman army insured this peace, called the *Pax Romana*.

5. Worldwide degeneration:

    > "The world was in a state of extraordinary moral degeneration. Two thousand lords in Rome had 1,300,000 slaves, which were treated with great cruelty. In the empire, there were 6,000,000 slaves. The rich lived in the utmost profligacy. Chastity and marriage were the exception while divorce and immorality were the rule. The priests preyed upon the masses of the ignorant. Many seductive cults exerted a degrading influence. The religion of the Romans had no power to cope with the degeneracy of the times. The philosophies of the Greeks failed. None of the philosophies could meet the deep moral needs of the times. The emperors were monsters of crime. Thousands of lives were sacrificed in the arena to furnish entertainment for the emperor and a bloodthirsty population. Luxury was beyond description. The horrible character of vice and crime is witnessed by the excavated objects of Pompeii. Seneca testified that children were considered with great disfavor and infant exposure was prevalent. Tacitus said that the spirit of the times was 'to corrupt and to be corrupted.' Paul gives a picture in the Roman epistle of a people who had departed from the God revealed in nature and conscience, to set up for themselves, through vain independence, gods like unto creatures. From this idol worship they had gone on into moral degeneracy and

crime until they were lost in a world of darkness and destruction. This was the condition of the world morally when Jesus came, who was to 'overcome the world' with His gospel."[8]

6. Intermingling of world religions:

"And now there came a migration of gods and idols from the Orient, a mixing and fusing of religions and cults, which in its 'Babylonian' confusion of deities stands quite unique in human history. State gods, Greek gods, gods from the Orient, with mixed religion and mysteries, blended ever more into a single, many-colored, mighty, main river. Religiously, the east conquered the west. Rome became a venerator of all deities, often horribly grotesque, senselessly confused, ill-formed, sickly fantasies. The entire Mediterranean world resembled a gigantic cauldron of mixture. A western-eastern religious chaos, without parallel, has arisen. The ancient religions went spiritually bankrupt. But in this very feature they revealed the overruling of the redeemer God preparing beforehand His salvation."[9]

Jesus Christ came into the world to work and teach, laying the foundation of His Church (Matt. 16:18).

The Gospels record three main areas of Christ's work: (1) His miracles, (2) His training of the twelve disciples, and (3) His sacrifice on the Cross to provide redemption.

Miracles- Jesus used miracles to prove that He was God. Jesus healed people of physical illness (Isa. 35:5; 61:1; John 5:1-18) and performed miracles that demonstrated His power over nature (John 2:11; Mark 4:39-41). He also delivered people from demonic possession and oppression (Matt. 8:28-34), demonstrating His power over the supernatural. Finally, he demonstrated His power over death itself by raising people from the dead (John 11:38-44; Mark 5:41).

Training- Jesus specifically chose twelve men whom he would prepare to take His message throughout the world (Luke 6:12-13). Mark 3:14 explains that Jesus appointed these men to be "with Him" and "sent out to preach." At the end of His earthly ministry, after choosing and training His disciples, Jesus commissioned them:

"Go ye therefore, and teach all nations, baptizing them in the name of the Father, and of the Son, and of the Holy Ghost:

---

[8] J.W. Shepard, *The Christ of the Gospels.*
[9] Erich Sauer, *The Dawn of World Redemption.*

*teaching them to observe all things whatsoever I have
commanded you: and, lo, I am with you alway, even unto the
end of the world." –Matt. 28:19-20*

The disciples were to be (1) going, (2) baptizing and (3) teaching.

Words Used with "Going" in the New Testament	
Greek Word	**Meaning**
diangello	"to announce"
katangello	"to tell thoroughly, by comparison"
euangelizo	"to spread good news"
laleo	"to talk or speak conversationally"
kerusso	"to herald or proclaim, to preach"

The Disciples' Commission	
Going	Taking the "good news" of Jesus Christ and sharing it with the world.
Baptizing	Separating from the old life and old relationships to enter the new, living way of walking in the Spirit (Rom. 6; 1 Pet. 3:21). This securing of commitment was like the *eperotema*— the oath of allegiance a Roman soldier took to serve and defend the empire.
Teaching	Renewing the Mind through the Word of God in order to "observe to do" God's will as we grow in grace and the knowledge of Jesus Christ our Lord.

Redemption- Through His sacrifice on the Cross for the sins of the whole world and his resurrection from death, Jesus secured the eternal redemption of all who will receive Him personally. Christ's greatest work was his faithfulness to God's plan of redemption. He gave His life as a voluntary, substitutionary sacrifice for the sin of the human race (2 Cor. 5:21). The Gospel of John explains that Jesus is the Eternal Word of God (John 1:1-5), and we must either receive or reject Him (John 1:9-13, 14:6). According to John 1:18, Jesus makes God known. John 1:29 describes Him as the Lamb of God. We must believe in Him for eternal life (John. 3:16), because He alone has eternal life (John 5:25) and eternal life is in His name (John 20:31).

The coming of Jesus Christ was the greatest moment in history. God Himself came to earth and gave Himself to redeem mankind. It was the greatest act of love ever imaginable. The great need for reconciliation between man and God that the Old Testament saints anticipated was completely fulfilled in Christ. This redemption is the turning point of human history.

In his Gospel account, Luke captures the emotion of this epic moment in his portrait of Simeon:

> *"And, behold, there was a man in Jerusalem, whose name was Simeon; and the same man was just and devout, waiting for the consolation of Israel: and the Holy Ghost was upon him. And it was revealed unto him by the Holy Ghost, that he should not see death, before he had seen the Lord's Christ. And he came by the Spirit into the temple: and when the parents brought in the child Jesus, to do for him after the custom of the law, Then took he him up in his arms, and blessed God, and said, Lord, now lettest thou thy servant depart in peace, according to thy word: For mine eyes have seen thy salvation, Which thou hast prepared before the face of all people; A light to lighten the Gentiles, and the glory of thy people Israel." –Luke 2:25-32*

Since the Redeemer's coming, God's people no longer have to wait for reconciliation with God, we have it! And we have this message— the "good news" of redemption through Jesus Christ—to carry to the world.

> *"Moreover, brethren, I declare to you the gospel...that Christ died for our sins according to the Scriptures, and that He was buried, and that He rose again the third day according to the Scriptures." –1 Cor. 15:1-4*

God Speaks: The Gospels
(Matthew—John)

In His arrival as the promised Messiah, Jesus inaugurated the New Covenant, beginning the fulfillment of Jeremiah's prophecy (Jer. 31:31; Matt. 26:28). In fulfillment of all of the various ways he had spoken in the past, God was now speaking in His Son (Heb. 1:1-3).

The Need: The need was to sum up all that God had said before and all that He would say in the future. Jesus Christ, God in human flesh, was the ultimate revelation of God to us. He sums up the Old Testament and proclaims what the future holds. Everything in the New Testament from Acts to Revelation is a development of what Christ spoke (Matt. 5:17; 7:24-29; John 1:18; 6:63; 7:46; 14:10, 24; 17:8). In addition to fulfilling the Old Testament, Christ also initiated the Church Age by teaching the disciples (Mt. 16:13-19) and promising to empower them with His Spirit (Jn. 14-16).

The Content: Christ's teachings fulfilled and clarified the past. He did not come to abolish the Mosaic Law, but to fulfill it (Matt. 5:17-18). This is seen in His teachings on the relationship between murder and its root of anger, and adultery and its root of lust (Matt. 5:21-28). Jesus Christ's teachings were, in turn, the seed thoughts for the teachings in the epistles. For example, compare Jesus teaching on love in John 13:34-35 with Paul's teaching in 1 Corinthians 13:1-7.

Christ's teachings about Himself:

- *I...am He*, the Messiah (John 4:26)
- *I am the Bread of Life* (John 6:35)
- *I am the Door* (John 10:9)
- *I am the Son of God* (John 10:36)
- *I am the Resurrection and the Life* (John 11:25)
- *I am the Way, the Truth, and the Life* (John 14:6)
- Before Abraham was, *I am* (John 8:58)
- *I am* with you always (Matt. 28:20)

The Method: At this point in the history of redemption, God did not merely speak through a man. He became a man to demonstrate and speak the truth to mankind. This is called the Incarnation (John 1:1; 14-18; Phil. 2:5-11).

The Response Required: The entire Bible witnesses of Christ and all people must come to Jesus Christ for salvation. He said, "You search the Scriptures, because you think that in them you have eternal life; and it is they that bear witness to Me; yet you refuse to come to Me that you may have life" (John 5:39-40). To know God and possess eternal life, we must receive Him (John 1:12), and follow Him. This means several things: (1) continuing in His Word (Jn. 8:31), (2) loving as He loved (John 13:34-35), (3) taking up our "cross" (Luke 9:23), (4) bearing fruit (John 15:8), (5) valuing Christ above other relationships (Luke 14:26), and (6) counting the cost of following Jesus Christ (Luke 14:27).

ACT FOUR

God builds
His Church, proclaiming
salvation to every nation.

The Book of Acts

Scene One:
The Promise of the Church (Matthew 16:13-18; 28:16-20)

Before the incarnation of Jesus Christ, many Jews expected that the coming of their Messiah would immediately lead to a glorious new kingdom of peace, prosperity and righteousness for Israel. This was not exactly how God's plan of redemption was to play out.

When Jesus asked His disciples how they perceived His identity Peter answered, "You are the Christ, the Son of the living God." Peter accurately recognized Jesus' title, but probably misunderstood its meaning. In His promise to David, the LORD spoke of a father-son relationship that would exist between Himself and David's descendants. In Jesus, Peter saw the Messianic figure who was the heir to David's throne.

But Jesus was not about to establish a political kingdom. He promised that, beginning with Peter and his confession of faith in Jesus as the Son of God, He would build a different kind of kingdom that all the spiritual forces of darkness could not prevent. He said, "I will build My church; and the gates of hell shall not prevail against it" (Matt. 16:13-18).

Before departing from the earth after His resurrection, Jesus the Messiah gave His disciples specific instructions that revealed His will for the ages that followed. His last recorded words before returning to the Father disclosed the next phase in the drama of redemption—the worldwide proclamation of the Gospel:

"Then the eleven disciples went away into Galilee, into a mountain where Jesus had appointed them. And when they saw him, they worshipped him: but some doubted. And Jesus came and spake unto them, saying, All power is given unto me in heaven and in earth. Go ye therefore, and teach all nations, baptizing them in the name of the Father, and of the Son, and of the Holy Ghost: Teaching them to observe all things whatsoever I have commanded you: and, lo, I am with you alway, even unto the end of the world. Amen." —Matt. 28:16-20

"But ye shall receive power after that the Holy Ghost is come upon you: and ye shall be witnesses unto me both in Jerusalem, and in all Judaea, and in Samaria, and unto the uttermost part of the earth." —Acts. 1:8

The climax of God's plan of redemption was the work of Jesus Christ on earth. Through His incarnation, sacrificial death, and resurrection, he bore the cost of redeeming mankind and secured deliverance for all who believe in Him.

Following the first coming of Christ and in anticipation of His second coming, the LORD's main concern is the proclamation of the transforming message of salvation in Jesus Christ and the coming of His kingdom. This is how He is moving toward the final fulfillment of His promises and His ultimate goal of filling the earth with the glory of His presence. Although the nation of Israel was intended by God to be a witness to the people of other nations, they were commanded to be unique and isolated, separate from other nations. If Gentiles were to become part of Israel's community of faith, they would need to become Jewish and leave their previous political ties behind. Israel was never commanded to go out and actively pursue these proselytes. In contrast, Jesus' command to the disciples was that they carry the good news of His salvation and proclaim it throughout the world.

He did not merely tell his followers to "go witnessing." Instead, he explained that when the Holy Spirit empowered them they would *be* witnesses of Him, from Jerusalem to the ends of the earth (Acts 1:8). Their essential identity was wrapped up in what Jesus accomplished. He promised to be with them as they went, and that He will continue working until the end of the age, bringing salvation to every individual who believes in Him.

Scene Two:
Israel Is Set Aside (Romans 9-11)

Although some Jews believed in Him, the political and religious establishment in Israel rejected the idea that Jesus was their Messiah. He was not the political leader they expected, nor was He sympathetic to their views. Because of its rejection of Jesus Christ, Israel as a nation has been temporarily set aside from God's redemptive program. Nevertheless, the Church of Jesus Christ is founded on the twelve apostles, all of whom were Jewish.

In Romans 9-11, Paul uses the image of the olive tree to illustrate the inclusion of the Gentiles as part of the people of God, the people of His redemptive program. The roots and trunk of the olive tree represent OT believers (Israel, cf. Jer. 11:16). The believing church, which has been grafted into this tree, now shares in the promises and plan of God for His people. This unity of the people of God as the olive tree does not erase the distinguishable aspects of Israel and the Church, nor does the continuity of God's redemptive program erase the distinguishable aspects of Israel and the Church in the kingdom of God. In other words, the Church has not replaced Israel.[10] Israel and the Church are distinguishable aspects of the one people and one redemptive program of God.

The book of Acts records the establishment of the Church as a non-political community of people who love and follow Jesus Christ. In contrast to Israel, whose identity as a nation required independence and separation from other nations, the Church must exist within another nation. A survey of Church History reveals that all attempts to establish the Church as a political entity have resulted in the failure of the Church's ministry. The Church is commanded to preach the Gospel, which requires that Christ's followers intermingle with those who have not yet believed the Gospel.

If Israel as a nation had tried to take the Gospel to other nations, it would have been a political invasion. The Church was better suited to proclaim the "whosoever" of John 3:16. Essentially, Israel was a passive witness for God. Once the political element was removed, the LORD's people could go to any nation as Christ's ambassadors without being seen as a political threat (cf. 1 Tim. 6).

---

[10] See Walter C. Kaiser, *The Promise-Plan of God: A Biblical Theology of the Old and New Testaments,* 25-29.

Comparing the Nation and the Church	
Nation	**Church**
Exclusive	Universal
National (Jewish)	International (Gentile)
One Particular Location	Local
Political	Non-political (1 Pet. 1:9-10)
A physical temple building	A temple of individuals

Figures Used to Describe the Church	
A Temple for God	Eph. 2:19-22; 1 Cor. 3:16, 6:19-20; 1 Pet. 2:5-6
The Body of Christ, the head	1 Cor. 12:12
The Flock of the Shepherd	Acts 20:28-29

Scene Three:
Jesus Builds His Church from the Seeds of Israel (Acts 1-12)

There are similarities between how God built a nation and how He builds the Church. The nation was founded on the twelve sons of Jacob, while Christ began building His Church with the twelve Apostles whom He chose. They asked Jesus to restore Israel's theocracy, but He deferred their request until the building of His Church is complete (Acts 1:1-14).

Acts 1

To empower His disciples and enable them to be His witnesses, God poured out His Holy Spirit while the disciples celebrated Pentecost (Acts 2:1-21). This visible, historical manifestation of the coming of the Holy Spirit to indwell and empower Jesus' followers had a specific goal: the proclamation of the Gospel to all nations.

Acts 2

Following Pentecost, the believers continued to worship at the Jerusalem temple. However, God wanted to move them out into the world. The temple was a feature of the religious-political entity of Israel. If the Church was to include people from all nations, it would have to move out to other lands.

Evidence of the Holy Spirit came not only through visible or audible phenomena like tongues of fire, rushing wind from heaven and the miraculous ability to speak in foreign languages, but also in the rapid growth of the Church in Jerusalem. This growth provided a strong base for the Church's spread out into other areas.

The Rapid Growth of the Early Church	
120 devoted to prayer	Acts 1:14-15
3,000 added in one day	Acts 2:41
5,000 men heard and believed	Acts 4:4
More multitudes of believers added	Acts 5:14
Disciples increased in number	Acts 6:1
The Church multiplied	Acts 9:31

Acts 8

The rapid growth of the Church was a threat to the Jewish establishment in Jerusalem. The Pharisees launched a full-scale assault on the followers of Christ. As a result, the apostles began to preach in areas outside of Jerusalem. Philip set an example for the other apostles, proclaiming Christ in Samaria and Gaza. The persecution caused the Gospel message to spread outside of Jerusalem.

Acts 9

Acts 10

The LORD chose Saul, the Pharisee who led the persecution against Christians, to become the apostle to the Gentiles. As He had done for the patriarchs in the Old Testament, the LORD gave Saul a new name (Paul) and a new identity as His messenger to the non-Jewish nations (Acts 9:15) of the world. Following Paul's conversion, the Jerusalem Church experienced peace once again. Through Paul, Peter and the other apostles, the door was opened for the Gentiles to be "grafted in" to the olive tree of God's people Israel (Acts 10:1-6; Rom. 11:17-24).

Acts 11

The first Gentile Christian congregation was established at Antioch of Syria (Acts 11:18-26). This great fellowship was the first place that followers of Christ were called "Christians." The Antioch church began to send men out to other cultures. And so, the Church developed from a small group of Jews in Jerusalem to a growing, multi-cultural, international fellowship with thousands of believers.

Scene Four:
The Gospel Goes to All Nations (Acts 13-28)

The proclamation of the Gospel of Jesus Christ began to be preached in Jerusalem, just as Jesus foretold:

> *"And he said unto them, These are the words which I spake unto you, while I was yet with you, that all things must be fulfilled, which were written in the law of Moses, and in the prophets, and in the psalms, concerning me. Then opened he their understanding, that they might understand the scriptures, And said unto them, Thus it is written, and thus it behoved Christ to suffer, and to rise from the dead the third day: And that repentance and remission of sins should be preached in his name among all nations, beginning at Jerusalem. And ye are witnesses of these things." –Lk. 24:44-48*

After the Jewish persecution of Christians in Jerusalem caused the Gospel to spread to Samaria, and from Samaria to the Gentile center of Syrian Antioch, the LORD appointed Paul and Barnabas to carry the message of Christ throughout the rest of the first-century Mediterranean world. As the believers in Antioch fasted and prayed, they heard the Holy Spirit speak, saying, "Separate me Barnabas and Saul for the work whereunto I have called them" (Acts 13:3).

Acts 13

On their first missionary journey (Acts 13-14), Paul and Barnabas took the message to the Jews first, presenting Christ as the fulfillment of the Word of God in the Jewish synagogues wherever they went (Acts 13:4-5). Most of the Jews rejected the idea that Jesus was their long-awaited Messiah, so Paul and Barnabas took the message to the Gentiles, who received it happily. As they preached in the city of Iconium, unbelieving Jews incited violence against Paul and Barnabas. At Lystra they stoned Paul and left him for dead. Even this could not stop Paul's zeal to see believers established in their new identity as the body of Jesus Christ. He and Barnabas appointed elders to provide leadership for the new believers in every place they preached.

Paul selected Timothy to travel with him on his second missionary journey (Acts 15:26—18:21). Their main goal was to strengthen the churches that had been established during the first missionary journey (Acts 16:4-5). During the second journey, they encountered the noble people of Berea who set a high standard for all Christians as they "searched the Scriptures daily" to see if the message that Paul was preaching was indeed the truth (Acts 17:11).

Acts 15

Acts 18

On his third missionary journey, Paul strengthened the disciples (Acts 18:22-23) and reached all of Asia with the message of Christ's suffering and resurrection. The end of the book of Acts records Paul under house arrest in Rome. Despite his incarceration, he was "preaching the kingdom of God, and teaching those things which concern the Lord Jesus Christ, with all confidence, no man forbidding him" (Acts 28:31).

Acts 28

Christ's command to reach the entire world with the "good news" of His redemption is called "The Great Commission" (Matt. 28:18-19). It will continue to be in effect until the Rapture when Jesus comes to receive His bride, the Church. The LORD is working all over the world, and when the whole world is reached with the Gospel, the end of this period of history will come. In the book of Acts, however, we can see how the words of Jesus Christ in Acts 1:8 were literally fulfilled:

The Spread of the Gospel in Acts	
To Jerusalem	Acts 1:1-6:7
To Palestine	Acts 6:8-9:31
To Syria	Acts 9:32-12:24
To Asia Minor	Acts 12:25-16:5
To Europe	Acts 16:6-19:20
To Rome (the uttermost parts)	Acts 19:21-28:31

The Six Progress Reports in Acts	
Acts 1:1-6:7	Word kept spreading, disciples increased in Jerusalem, and many priests were becoming obedient to the faith.
Acts 6:8-9:31	The church throughout Judea, Galilee, Samaria was being built up and continuing in the fear of the Lord and the comfort of the Holy Spirit.
Acts 9:32-12:24	Herod, the political leader, died, "But the Word of the Lord continued to grow and to be multiplied."
Acts 12:25-16:5	After the first missionary journey and the council at Jerusalem, Paul and Barnabas separated, but "The churches were being strengthened in the faith and increasing numbers daily."
Acts 16:6-19:20	The church overcame magic practices and books priced at 50,000 pieces of silver were burned, "So the word of the Lord was growing mightily and prevailing."
Acts 19:21-28:31	Paul carried the gospel to Rome, preaching and teaching Jesus with all openness, unhindered.

Insights on Missions from the Book of Acts
The church as a whole was a missionary society.
Paul chose strategic places; centers like Antioch, Corinth, Ephesus, Athens and Rome.
Churches were established to be self-governing, self-supporting and self-perpetuating to extend out the gospel.

God Speaks: The Epistles
(Romans—Jude)

The Epistles were written to those who (1) heard the gospel and believed unto salvation (Eph. 1:13a), (2) were filled with the Spirit (Eph. 1:13b-14) and had the gifts of the Spirit (1 Cor. 1:7), and (3) were witnessing with power (1 Thess. 1:8).

The Need: The need was twofold: (1) they needed to understand the essential nature of salvation, and (2) they needed to know how to work out the Gospel in life and service. The Epistles, written as personal letters, explain the beauty of the Christian life and its responsibilities.

The Content: The foundational concept of the Epistles is that this new salvation is anchored in a new relationship with a risen Savior. The source of this new life is in Christ, not in us. The believer must learn that he or she is united with Him. The phrase "in Christ" is found throughout Paul's epistles. This phrase captures the truth of our union with Christ. 1 Corinthians 1:31 states that Christ is our wisdom, justification, sanctification, service and glorification. The Epistles deal with every kind of problem that believers will face: (1) basic issues are dealt with in Romans and 1 & 2 Corinthians, (2) life problems are addressed in Paul's epistles and the general epistles, and (3) pastoral problems are conquered in 1 & 2 Timothy and Titus.

The Method: The method was teaching through letters. These letters are explanatory, developing the blessings, implications and obligations that are part of life "in Christ". God is concerned with developing the spiritual life of the believers. He wants us to grow in maturity. The epistolary form personalizes the doctrine that needed to be communicated.

The Response Required: Appropriate, by faith, Christ!

ACT FIVE

God fills the earth
with His glory.

Revelation

Scene One:
The Promise of Israel's Complete Restoration
(Jeremiah, Ezekiel & Amos)

Despite its failure to recognize Jesus as its Messiah, the nation of Israel has not been permanently removed from God's redemptive program. The LORD described his covenant with Israel as an everlasting covenant:

> "For thus saith the Lord GOD; I will even deal with thee as thou hast done, which hast despised the oath in breaking the covenant. Nevertheless I will remember my covenant with thee in the days of thy youth, and I will establish unto thee an everlasting covenant." –Ezek. 16:59-60

Since the first coming of Jesus Christ, Israel has been set aside so that the rest of the nations of the world could become part of the community of God's redeemed people, as the LORD's promise to one nation became a universal message of salvation for all nations:

> "For I would not, brethren, that ye should be ignorant of this mystery, lest ye should be wise in your own conceits; that blindness in part is happened to Israel, until the fulness of the Gentiles be come in. And so all Israel shall be saved: as it is written, There shall come out of Sion the Deliverer, and shall turn away ungodliness from Jacob: For this is my covenant unto them, when I shall take away their sins. As concerning the gospel, they are enemies for your sakes: but as touching the election, they are beloved for the fathers' sakes. For the gifts and calling of God are without repentance." –Rom. 11:25-28

Because Israel rejected Christ at His first coming, some have concluded that the nation permanently forfeited all of its promises and blessings to the Gentiles. But the prophets of the Old Testament clearly foretold that Israel's theocracy would be permanently restored and all of the LORD's promises to the nation would one day be fulfilled:

> "Behold, the days come, saith the LORD, that I will make a new covenant with the house of Israel...I will put my law in their inward parts, and write it in their hearts; and will be their God, and they shall be my people. And they shall teach no more every man his neighbour, and every man his brother, saying, Know the LORD: for they shall all know me, from the least of them unto the greatest of them, saith the LORD: for I will forgive their iniquity, and I will remember their sin no more. Thus saith the LORD, which giveth the sun for a light by day, and the

*ordinances of the moon and of the stars for a light by night,
which divideth the sea when the waves thereof roar; The LORD
of hosts is his name: If those ordinances depart from before me,
saith the LORD, then the seed of Israel also shall cease from
being a nation before me for ever...Behold, the days come, saith
the LORD, that the city shall be built to the LORD...it shall not be
plucked up, nor thrown down any more for ever." –Jer. 31:31-
40*

*"For I will take you from among the heathen, and gather you out
of all countries, and will bring you into your own land. Then will
I sprinkle clean water upon you, and ye shall be clean: from all
your filthiness, and from all your idols, will I cleanse you. A new
heart also will I give you, and a new spirit will I put within you:
and I will take away the stony heart out of your flesh, and I will
give you an heart of flesh. And I will put my spirit within you,
and cause you to walk in my statutes, and ye shall keep my
judgments, and do them. And ye shall dwell in the land that I
gave to your fathers; and ye shall be my people, and I will be
your God. I will also save you from all your uncleannesses: and I
will call for the corn, and will increase it, and lay no famine
upon you. And I will multiply the fruit of the tree, and the
increase of the field, that ye shall receive no more reproach of
famine among the heathen." –Ezek. 36:24-30*

*"In that day will I raise up the tabernacle of David that is fallen,
and close up the breaches thereof; and I will raise up his ruins,
and I will build it as in the days of old: That they may possess the
remnant of Edom, and of all the heathen, which are called by my
name, saith the LORD that doeth this. Behold, the days come,
saith the LORD, that the plowman shall overtake the reaper, and
the treader of grapes him that soweth seed; and the mountains
shall drop sweet wine, and all the hills shall melt. And I will
bring again the captivity of my people of Israel, and they shall
build the waste cities, and inhabit them; and they shall plant
vineyards, and drink the wine thereof; they shall also make
gardens, and eat the fruit of them. And I will plant them upon
their land, and they shall no more be pulled up out of their land
which I have given them, saith the LORD thy God." –Amos 9:11-
15*

The fulfillment of God's plan of redemption will include the
restored nation of Israel. According to Scripture, there will come a
day when the blessings of the nation of Israel will be restored, never
to be lost again. Unlike the restoration following the Babylonian
captivity, this restoration will be complete and permanent, after the
"full number of the Gentiles" has become part of the redeemed
people of God.

Revelation's Seven Beatitudes	
1:3	*"Blessed is he that readeth, and they that hear the words of this prophecy, and keep those things which are written therein: for the time is at hand."*
14:13	*"And I heard a voice from heaven saying unto me, Write, 'Blessed are the dead which die in the Lord from henceforth: Yea, saith the Spirit, that they may rest from their labours; and their works do follow them.'"*
16:15	*"Behold, I come as a thief. Blessed is he that watcheth, and keepeth his garments, lest he walk naked, and they see his shame."*
19:9	*"And he saith unto me, 'Write, Blessed are they which are called unto the marriage supper of the Lamb. And he saith unto me, These are the true sayings of God.'"*
20:6	*"Blessed and holy is he that hath part in the first resurrection: on such the second death hath no power, but they shall be priests of God and of Christ, and shall reign with him a thousand years."*
22:7	*"Behold, I come quickly: blessed is he that keepeth the sayings of the prophecy of this book."*
22:14	*"Blessed are they that do his commandments, that they may have right to the tree of life, and may enter in through the gates into the city."*

Scene Two:
The Church is Removed (1 Thessalonians 4:13-18)

The prophets of the Old Testament and the writers of the New Testament foretold the great Day of the LORD, a period of time comprised of several events: the Rapture, the appearance of the "man of sin" (2 Thess. 2), the Great Tribulation, the second coming of Christ, the establishment of the Millennial Reign of Christ, the Last Judgment and the creation of the New Heaven and New Earth.

Before the final return of Jesus Christ to the earth, the Church will be removed from amongst the enemies of God and meet the Lord Jesus in the air. This display of Christ's power as He delivers His people is called the Rapture:

> "For the Lord himself shall descend from heaven with a shout, with the voice of the archangel, and with the trump of God: and the dead in Christ shall rise first: Then we which are alive and remain shall be caught up together with them in the clouds, to meet the Lord in the air: and so shall we ever be with the Lord."
> −1 Thess. 4:16-17

The Rapture will occur when Christ's work of building His Church is complete. When the Church has been taken up to be with Christ forever, the focus of God's program will turn back to the final fulfillment of God's promise to fill the earth with His glory through the restored nation of Israel.

Scene Three:
The Great Tribulation (Revelation 6—18)

The time period that precedes the Second Coming of Jesus Christ will be difficult for the nation of Israel. In fact, Jesus Himself foretold that the Great Tribulation will be the worst time of suffering the world has ever seen—even worse than Israel's deportations to Assyria and Babylon (Matt. 21:24). As terrible as the Great Tribulation will be, it will also signal the nearness of Christ's glorious return. After he told His disciples about the Great Tribulation and the signs that will mark the end of this present age, Jesus said:

Rev. 6

> *"And when these things begin to come to pass, then look up, and lift up your heads; for your redemption draweth nigh."* —Luke 21:28

Even before the first coming of Christ, the prophets of the LORD predicted both the future tribulation and spiritual restoration of Israel. Jeremiah spoke of the Great Tribulation calling it the "time of Jacob's trouble." He also prophesied that after this time of suffering, the LORD would deliver Israel and restore it to its Davidic king (Jer. 30:1-9). The prophet Daniel also prophesied about this time period, including details about a sinister "prince" who would defile the Jewish temple with a detestable sacrifice (Dan. 7:21ff; 9:24-27).

The Great Tribulation will be a horrible time, largely because of the great deception that will come upon the world. A false messiah will arise, blaspheming against God and convincing the nations of the world that he, and not Jesus Christ, is their long-awaited ruler. Through this Great Tribulation, Israel will be prepared to see Jesus Christ return, this time as their glorious Davidic ruler, the true Messiah they have been waiting for.

Scene Four:
The Coming of the King (Revelation 11:15; 19:1-21)

The Gospel of Matthew portrays Jesus Christ as King (Matt. 2:2; 27:22-27). At His First Coming, only a few recognized Jesus as their King. At His Second Coming, however, all people will see His glorious arrival and all will know that Jesus is the rightful King of the world.

Jeremiah's prophecy of the Righteous Branch of David foretold Christ's coming to reign on earth:

> *"Behold, the days come, saith the LORD, that I will raise unto David a righteous Branch, and a King shall reign and prosper, and shall execute judgment and justice in the earth. In his days Judah shall be saved, and Israel shall dwell safely: and this is his name whereby he shall be called, THE LORD OUR RIGHTEOUSNESS." –Jer. 23:5-6*

Daniel also described the Messiah's reign as an "everlasting kingdom":

> *"I saw in the night visions, and, behold, one like the Son of man came with the clouds of heaven, and came to the Ancient of days, and they brought him near before him. And there was given him dominion, and glory, and a kingdom, that all people, nations, and languages, should serve him: his dominion is an everlasting dominion, which shall not pass away, and his kingdom that which shall not be destroyed." –Dan. 7:13-14*

Rev. 11   John's entire vision of the last days is called "The Revelation of Jesus Christ." John saw ahead to the moment when Jesus will finally be revealed as the everlasting Ruler of the earth:

> *"And the seventh angel sounded; and there were great voices in heaven, saying, The kingdoms of this world are become the kingdoms of our Lord, and of his Christ; and he shall reign for ever and ever." –Rev. 11:15*

Rev. 19   When Christ returns to rule the earth at the end of the Great Tribulation, all the nations of the earth who oppose His kingdom will gather against Him at the Battle of Armageddon (Zech. 14:1-15; Rev. 19:11-21). But Jesus Christ will decimate His enemies' army using only His Word; the same Word that created the universe in the beginning (Rev. 19:21; cf. Gen. 1:1-31 and Jn. 1:1-3). Then Christ will reign over the whole earth from Israel, fulfilling the LORD's words in Psalm 2:

"Why do the heathen rage, and the people imagine a vain thing? The kings of the earth set themselves, and the rulers take counsel together, against the LORD, and against his anointed, saying, Let us break their bands asunder, and cast away their cords from us. He that sitteth in the heavens shall laugh: the Lord shall have them in derision. Then shall he speak unto them in his wrath, and vex them in his sore displeasure. Yet have I set my king upon my holy hill of Zion." —Ps. 2:1-6

Scene Five:
The Millennial Kingdom (Revelation 20)

Rev. 20

Jesus Christ's victory over His enemies will culminate when Satan himself, whose deception in the Garden of Eden marked the beginning of humanity's corruption, will be bound and thrown into an abyss called the "bottomless pit". As long as he is imprisoned there, it will be impossible for Satan to deceive the inhabitants of Christ's kingdom (Rev. 20:1-3).

With Satan imprisoned and all the nations of the earth subject to Jesus Christ, the resurrected saints will enjoy a thousand years of peace under the theocracy of the great King from David's lineage who is the Son of God. Jesus Christ the Messiah will rule from Jerusalem and all of the LORD's promises to Israel will be fulfilled (Rev. 20:4-6).

What will the LORD do through Israel in Act 5?	
Rom. 11:15	Their acceptance will mean life from the dead.
Is. 2:2-4	Israel will be over all nations.
Gen. 12:3	The LORD will bless those who bless Israel and curse those who curse Israel.
Gen. 12:3	The LORD will bless all the families of the earth through Israel, which is Abraham's seed.
Is. 60:3	The nations will come to Israel's light.
Num. 14:21; Rev. 21:23	The glory of the LORD will fill the earth from Jerusalem.

For reasons that are not disclosed in the Scriptures, Satan will be released from his imprisonment in the bottomless pit at the end of the thousand-year reign of Christ. He will go out deceiving the nations of the world and amass an international army of people who rebel against the Messiah's kingdom. This army of "Gog and Magog" (different from Ezekiel 38-39) will besiege Jerusalem, the beloved city of Christ. Fire will descend from heaven and consume them, and Satan will be thrown into the lake of fire where the beast and the false prophet (of Rev. 13) already await him (Rev. 20:7-10). After the fiery judgment of God has destroyed Satan's army and Satan has been judged, all the dead of the ages (those who did not take part in the first resurrection) will be summoned to appear before Christ at the Great White Throne. At this final, dreadful trial, people will be judged and condemned according to what they did during their lives on earth. When these events are complete, the unrepentant enemies of Christ will be forever defeated and separated from God and His kingdom.

Epilogue:
The New Heaven and the New Earth (Revelation 21-22)

Rev. 21

The last two chapters of the Bible reveal that the world we now know will not remain as it is forever. Our present heaven and earth will pass away and make way for the New Heaven and New Earth, which God has designed. John's vision of this new creation provides one of the most beautiful paragraphs in the Bible:

> *"And I saw a new heaven and a new earth: for the first heaven and the first earth were passed away; and there was no more sea. And I John saw the holy city, new Jerusalem, coming down from God out of heaven, prepared as a bride adorned for her husband. And I heard a great voice out of heaven saying, Behold, the tabernacle of God is with men, and he will dwell with them, and they shall be his people, and God himself shall be with them, and be their God. And God shall wipe away all tears from their eyes; and there shall be no more death, neither sorrow, nor crying, neither shall there be any more pain: for the former things are passed away."* –Rev. 21:1-4

Rev. 22

In these chapters (and in Is. 65:17, 66:22, and 2 Pet. 3:10-13) there is no description of exactly how God will create this new world, but John does receive a clear picture of the most important feature of the New Jerusalem: God Himself will dwell with His people there. The New Heaven and New Earth will be defined by the glory of the unmediated presence of God in the New Jerusalem. God's dimension (heaven) and ours (earth) will finally come together, without any sin in between. There will be no need for a temple and no need for the sun or the moon. The gates of the city will never be shut. In this New Jerusalem, the redeemed of every nation, tribe, people and language will enjoy the greatest gift that could ever be given: pure fellowship with the LORD. And all those who have been saved throughout all the ages of the earth will live forever worshipping in the glory of the awesome presence of the LORD, the Creator and Redeemer of humanity.

God Speaks: The Revelation of Jesus Christ
(Revelation)

This is God's final word to man in the Scriptures. It was given to encourage faithful believers and to reveal the final fulfillment of God's plan for history when he will consummate all things through Jesus Christ's physical return to earth. This is a book of prophecy and it is full of symbolism. The symbols have assigned meanings, and nearly all of them are rooted in the Old Testament.

The Need: Because of all the evil in the world and great opposition to the Church and its faith in Christ, Christians need assurance that Jesus Christ and His people will eventually win the spiritual war that has raged since the fall of mankind. This book proclaims the victory of Jesus Christ.

The Content:

    I.   The Person of Christ in Glorified Power: Chapter 1
    II. The People of Christ in the Church on Earth: Chapters 2 & 3
    III. The Christ's Program from Heaven's Viewpoint: Chapters 4-22
          A. The Worship of God in Heaven: Chapters 4 & 5
          B. The Great Tribulation in the World: Chapters 6-18
          C. The Return of Christ to Reign: Chapter 19
          D. The Millennium Kingdom of Christ: Chapter 20
          E. The Eternal State Revealed: Chapters 21 & 22

The Method: This book was given by Jesus Christ through angelic messengers to the Apostle John. Only the child of God will appreciate its spiritual message which is communicated through symbolic language. However, its message of Jesus Christ's victory and His restoration of all creation is no myth. This inspired message will truly take place in actual history. It is to be received as an encouragement to persevere and trust God through every challenge and trial with total commitment to Jesus Christ, until He comes and we live with Him forever.

The Response Required: "Look up for your redemption draws near" (Luke 21:28) and "Be faithful...even unto death" (Rev. 2:10; 12:11).

CONCLUSION

From Genesis to Revelation, the Bible tells the story of the one true God and his mighty work of redemption. It is the most beautiful story that has ever been told. And, best of all, this story is true. The events the Bible records are not fictional, they really happened. Realizing this causes us to feel the full importance of this great drama of redemption. If we actually believe it—that God chose a nation, that He judged and restored that nation, that He came and lived on this earth, that He is alive and working today, and that He will come again—then we know what significance, purpose and direction God has for our lives. As we wait for Christ's Second Coming, God wants the transformative message of His redemption in Jesus Christ to be proclaimed throughout the world.

The Gospel of Luke tells the story of the prophetess Anna and her first encounter with Jesus, who at the time was a small baby being presented at the temple. When she saw the little child and recognized that He was her long-awaited Messiah, the Scripture says, "That instant she gave thanks to the Lord, and spoke of Him to all those who looked for redemption in Jerusalem" (Luke 2:38). When we recognize Jesus as the Redeemer, we also ought to give humble thanks to God, and proclaim His redemption to everyone we can reach.

If you are not yet a believer in Jesus Christ, we hope this study has clearly presented the truth about who He is. We also hope that you will consider committing your life to Him, and begin to experience the joy of His redeeming love for you.

And if you have believed in Him, we trust that this simple study of His story, the drama of redemption, has motivated and encouraged you to know Him more fully, to love Him more fervently, and to serve Him more faithfully as you reach others with His love.

APPENDIX A: FOR FURTHER REFLECTION

Jesus Christ was **vicariously** wounded for our transgressions; bruised ˙ for our iniquities; the chastisement of our peace was upon Him; with His stripes we are healed; the Lord laid on Him the iniquity of us all; so Him who knew no sin was made sin on our behalf; because in His own self He bore our sins in His body upon the tree; so Christ died as the Passover lamb, the true Sin-offering, for our sins according to the Scriptures (1 Cor. 15:3).

His **substitutionary** death was to our great advantage; that He might bring us to God. He has reconciled us to the extent that God, through the propitiatory blood sprinkled on heaven's mercy seat, has turned His holy face toward man. The blood of the only One who perfectly kept God's holy law, made **atonement** and covered over all of its demands, blotting out our transgressions, and releasing us so completely that there is now no condemnation to those who are in Christ Jesus. The just demands of God are **satisfied** in and through Him alone.

Redemption centers around the debt we owed and the price He paid to **release** us from that indebtedness. The Greek word meaning simply "payment" or "price" is *misthos*. There is another word which means to pay a price that effects a ransom or **deliverance** to the extent of setting a prisoner free; that word is *lutron*. "Jesus Christ gave His life a **ransom**," a *lutron* (Mk. 10:45; Mt. 20:28); and an *antilutron*, an antidote or remedy for the poisonous disease of sin (1 Ti. 2:6). The story of Redemption must declare not only the price paid but to what extent we have been **set free** by that price; and that extent is directly related to the uniqueness of the Redeemer Himself and His relationship to God.

Since or because He was the fullness of the Godhead in bodily form, the only begotten Son of God, then His death upon the cross reveals the length, depth, width, and height of the righteous and holy love of God; and His bodily resurrection lifts our heads up in the sure hope of a full eternal redemption of spirit, soul and body. It has often been said that God has redeemed or delivered us from the **penalty**, is delivering us from the **power**, and will ultimately deliver us from the **presence** of sin.

His **eternal purpose** in redemption is seen in our conformity to the image of His Son (Rom. 8:29). Redemption causes us "to be filled up to all the fullness of God" (Eph. 3:19). Our capacity, created in the image of God, is to experience His eternal life; the life He came to give "abundantly" (Jn. 10:10); qualitative life in the superlative realm of His glory. What liberty, what freedom, what potential life you have if you enter into a right relationship with God, freely by His grace, through the redemption which is in Christ Jesus (Rom. 3:24)!

We pray that you receive by faith the redemption that is in Christ Jesus and **be fully restored** to God. As the Cross reveals God's unchanging heart of love toward you, may that Cross-love change and open your heart to the fellowship you were created for.

APPENDIX B: CHRIST IN THE BIBLE

Christ is the theme of the eight sections of the Bible:

Christ in the Eight Sections of the Bible	
The Law (Genesis—Deuteronomy)	The Foundation is laid for Christ
History (Joshua—Esther)	Preparation for Christ
Poetry (Job—Song of Songs)	Aspiration for Christ is Expressed
Prophecy (Isaiah—Malachi)	Expectation of Christ
Gospels (Matthew—John)	Manifestation of Christ
Acts	Proclamation of Christ
Epistles (Romans—Jude)	Interpretation and Application of Christ
Revelation	Consummation of All Things in Christ

Since Jesus Christ came to the earth, we are now able to see how all of Scripture finds its fulfillment in Him. The following Scripture references show some of the ways in which the nature of Jesus Christ is reflected in each of the sixty-six books of the Bible:

Christ in the Sixty-six Books of the Bible	
The Seed of the Woman	*"And I will put enmity between thee and the woman, and between thy seed and her seed; it shall bruise thy head, and thou shalt bruise its heel." –Gen. 3:15*
The Passover Lamb	*"Speak ye unto all the congregation of Israel, saying, In the tenth day of this month they shall take to hem every man a lamb, according to the house of their fathers, a lamb for an house." – Ex. 12:3*
The Atoning Sacrifice	*"For the life of the flesh is in the blood: and I have given it to you upon the altar to make an atonement for your souls: for it is the blood that maketh an atonement for the soul." –Lev. 17:11*
The Smitten Rock	*"Take the rod, and gather thou the assembly together, thou, and Aaron thy brother, and speak ye unto the rock before their eyes; and it shall give forth his water, and thou shalt bring forth to them water out of the rock: so thou shalt give the congregation and their beasts drink...And Moses lifted up his hand, and with his rod he smote the rock twice: and the water came out abundantly, and the congregation drank, and their beasts also." –Num. 20:8, 11*
The Faithful Prophet	*"I will raise them up a Prophet from among their brethren, like unto thee, and will put my words in his mouth; and he shall speak unto them all that I shall command him." –Deut. 18:18*
The Captain of the Lord's Army	*"And the captain of the LORD's host said unto Joshua, Loose thy shoe from off thy foot; for the place whereon thou standest is holy. And Joshua did so." –Josh. 5:15*

The Divine Deliverer	"And when the LORD raised them up judges, then the LORD was with the judge, and delivered them out of the hand of their enemies all the days of the judge: for it repented the LORD because of their groanings by reason of them that oppressed them and vexed them." – Judg. 2:18
The Kinsman Redeemer	"And now it is true that I am thy near kinsman: howbeit there is a kinsman nearer than I." – Ruth 3:12
The Anointed One	"The adversaries of the LORD shall be broken to pieces; out of heaven shall he thunder upon them: the LORD shall judge the ends of the earth; and he shall give strength unto his king, and exalt the horn of his anointed." –1 Sam. 2:10
The Son of David	"I will be his father, and he shall be my son. If he commit iniquity, I will chasten him with the rod of men, and with the stripes of the children of men." –2 Sam. 7:14
The Coming King	1 & 2 Kings
The Builder of the Temple	"And David said to Solomon his son, Be strong and of good courage, and do it: fear not, nor be dismayed: for the LORD God, even my God, will be with thee; he will not fail thee, nor forsake thee, until thou hast finished all the work for the service of the house of the LORD." –1 Chron. 28:20
The Restorer of the Temple	"And the elders of the Jews builded and they prospered through the prophesying of Haggai the prophet and Zechariah the son of Iddo. And they builded, and finished it, according to the commandment of the God of Israel, and according to the commandment of Cyrus, and Darius, and Artaxerxes king of Persia. And this house was finished on the third day of the month Adar, which was the sixth year of the reign of Darius the king." –Ezra 6:14, 15

The Restorer of the Nation	*"So the wall was finished in the twenty and fifth day of the month of Elul, in fifty and two days."* –Neh. 6:15
The Preserver of the Nation	*"For if thou altogether holdest thy peace at this time, then shall there enlargement and deliverance arise to the Jews from another place; but thou and thy father's house shall be destroyed: and who knoweth whether thou art come to the kingdom for such a time as this?"* – Esth. 4:14
The Living Redeemer	*"For I know that my redeemer liveth, and that he shall stand at the latter day upon the earth."* –Job 19:25
The Praise of Israel	*"Let every thing that hath breath praise the LORD. Praise ye the LORD."* –Psa. 150:6
The Wisdom of God	*"The LORD possessed me in the beginning of his way, before his works of old."* –Prov. 8:22, 23
The Great Teacher	*"The words of the wise are as goads, and as nails fastened by the masters of assemblies, which are given from one shepherd."* –Eccl. 12:11
The Fairest of Ten Thousand	*"My beloved is white and ruddy, the chiefest among ten thousand."* -Song 5:10
The Suffering Servant	*"He shall see of the travail of his soul, and shall be satisfied: by his knowledge shall my righteous servant justify many; for he shall bear their iniquities."* –Isa. 53:11
The Maker of the New Covenant	*"Behold, the days come, saith the LORD, that I will make a new covenant with the house of Israel, and with the house of Judah."* –Jer. 31:31

The Man of Sorrows	*"He sitteth alone and keepeth silence, because he hath borne it upon him. He putteth his mouth in the dust; if so be there may be hope. He giveth his cheek to him that smiteth him: he is filled full with reproach." –Lam. 3:28-30*
The Glory of God	*"And, behold, the glory of the God of Israel came from the way of the east: and his voice was like a noise of many waters: and the earth shined with his glory." –Ezek. 43:2*
The Coming Messiah	*"Know therefore and understand, that from the going forth of the commandment to restore and to build Jerusalem unto the Messiah the Prince shall be seven weeks, and threescore and two weeks: the street shall be built again, and the wall, even in troublous times." –Dan. 9:25*
The Lover of the Unfaithful	*"Then said the LORD unto me, Go yet, love a woman beloved of her friend, yet an adulteress, according to the love of the LORD toward the children of Israel, who look to other gods, and love flagons of wine." –Hos. 3:1*
The Hope of Israel	*"The LORD also shall roar out of Zion, and utter his voice from Jerusalem; and the heavens and the earth shall shake: but the LORD will be the hope of his people, and the strength of the children of Israel." –Joel 3:16*
The Husband-man	*"Behold, the days come, saith the LORD, that the plowman shall overtake the reaper, and the treader of grapes him that soweth seed; and the mountains shall drop sweet wine, and all the hills shall melt." –Amos 9:13*
The Savior	*"And saviours shall come up on mount Zion to judge the mount of Esau; and the kingdom shall be the LORD's." -Obad. 21*
The Resurrected One	*"And the LORD spake unto the fish, and it vomited out Jonah upon the dry land." –Jon. 2:10*

The Ruler in Israel	*"But thou, Bethlehem Ephratah, though thou be little among the thousands of Judah, yet out of thee shall he come forth unto me that is to be the ruler in Israel; whose goings forth have been from of old, from everlasting." –Mic. 5:2*
The Avenger	*"He that dasheth in pieces is come up before thy face: keep the munition, watch the way, make thy loins strong, fortify thy power mightily." – Nah. 2:1*
The Holy God	*"Thou art of purer eyes than to behold evil, and canst not look on iniquity: wherefore lookest thou upon them that deal treacherously, and holdest thy tongue when the wicked devoureth the man that is more righteous than he?" – Hab. 1:13*
The King of Israel	*"The LORD hath taken away thy judgments, he hath cast out thine enemy: the king of Israel, even the LORD, is in the midst of thee: thou shalt not see evil any more." –Zeph. 3:15*
The Desire of the Nation	*"And I will shake all nations, and the desire of all nations shall come: and I will fill this house with glory, saith the LORD of hosts." –Hag. 2:7*
The Righteous Branch	*"Hear now, O Joshua the high priest, thou, and thy fellows that sit before thee: for they are men wondered at: for, behold, I will bring forth my servant the BRANCH." –Zech. 3:8*
The Sun of Righteous- ness	*"But unto you that fear my name shall the Sun of righteousness arise with healing in his wings; and ye shall go forth, and grow up as calves of the stall." –Mal. 4:2*
The King of the Jews	*"Saying, Where is he that is born King of the Jews? for we have seen his star in the east, and are come to worship him." –Matt. 2:2*
The Servant of the LORD	*"For even the Son of man came not to be ministered unto, but to minister, and to give his life a ransom for many." –Mark 10:45*

The Son of Man	*"For the Son of man is come to seek and to save that which was lost." –Luke 19:10*
The Son of God	*"In the beginning was the Word, and the Word was with God, and the Word was God." –John. 1:1*
The Ascended Lord	*"And when he had spoken these things, while they beheld, he was taken up; and a cloud received him out of their sight." –Acts 1:10*
The Believer's Righteous- ness	*"For therein is the righteousness of God revealed from faith to faith: as it is written, The just shall live by faith." –Rom. 1:17*
The Believer's Sanctifica- tion	*"But of him are ye in Christ Jesus, who of God is made unto us wisdom, and righteousness, and sanctification, and redemption." –1 Cor. 1:30*
The Believer's Sufficiency	*"And he said unto me, My grace is sufficient for thee: for my strength is made perfect in weakness. Most gladly therefore will I rather glory in my infirmities, that the power of Christ may rest upon me." –2 Cor. 12:9*
The Believer's Liberty	*"And that because of false brethren unawares brought in, who came in privily to spy out our liberty which we have in Christ Jesus, that they might bring us into bondage." –Gal. 2:4*
The Exalted Head of the Church	*"And hath put all things under his feet, and gave him to be the head over all things to the church." –Eph. 1:22*
The Believer's Joy	*"That your rejoicing may be more abundant in Jesus Christ for me by my coming to you again." –Phil. 1:26*
The Fullness of Deity	*"For in him dwelleth all the fullness of the Godhead bodily." –Col. 2:9*

The Believer's Comfort	*"For the Lord himself shall descend from heaven with a shout, with the voice of the archangel, and with the trump of God: and the dead in Christ shall rise first: then we which are alive and remain shall be caught up together with them in the clouds, to meet the Lord in the air: and so shall we ever be with the Lord." –1 Thess. 4:16, 17*
The Believer's Glory	*"That the name of the Lord Jesus Christ may be glorified in you, and ye in him, according to the grace of our God and the Lord Jesus Christ." –2 Thess. 1:12*
The Believer's Preserver	*"For therefore we both labour and suffer reproach, because we trust in the living God, who is the Saviour of all men, specially of those that believe." –1 Tim. 4:10*
The Believer's Rewarder	*"Henceforth there is laid up for me a crown of righteousness, which the Lord, the righteous judge, shall give me at that day: and not to me only, but unto all them also that love his appearing." –2 Tim. 4:8*
The Blessed Hope	*"Looking for that blessed hope, and the glorious appearing of the great God and our Saviour Jesus Christ." –Tit. 2:13*
The Substitute	*"If thou count me therefore a partner, receive him as myself." –Philem. 17*
The High Priest	*"For we have not an high priest which cannot be touched with the feeling of our infirmities; but was in all points tempted like as we are, yet without sin." –Heb. 4:15*
The Giver of Wisdom	*"If any of you lack wisdom, let him ask of God, that giveth to all men liberally, and upbraideth not; and it shall be given him." –Jas. 1:5*
The Rock	*"Wherefore also it is contained in the scripture, Behold, I lay in Zion a chief cornerstone, elect, precious: and he that believeth on him shall not be confounded." –1 Pet. 2:6*

The Precious Promise	*"Whereby are given unto us exceeding great and precious promises: that by these ye might be partakers of the divine nature, having escaped the corruption that is in the world through lust." -2 Pet. 1:4*
The Life	*"He that hath the Son hath life; and he that hath not the Son of God hath not life." −1 Jn. 5:12*
The Truth	*"For the truth's sake, which dwelleth in us, and shall be with us for ever." −2 Jn. 2*
The Way	*"Beloved, follow not that which is evil, but that which is good." −3 Jn. 11*
The Believer's Advocate	*"Now unto him that is able to keep you from falling, and to present you faultless before the presence of his glory with exceeding joy, to the only wise God our Saviour, be glory and majesty, dominion and power, both now and ever. Amen." −Jude 24, 25*
The King of Kings and Lord of Lords	*"And he hath on his vesture and on his thigh a name written, KING OF KINGS, LORD OF LORDS." −Rev. 19:16*

APPENDIX C: THE UNITY OF THE BIBLE

Traditionally, there have been two major ways of viewing the unity of the Bible: covenant theology and dispensationalism. The following chart compares and contrasts these two approaches. It also describes how mediating views often combine elements from both systems of theology without fully embracing either approach.

Traditional Views on the Unity of the Bible		
Covenantal View	**Dispensational View**	**Mediating View**
Description: Covenant theology views God's relationship to humanity as a kind of agreement that governs God's dealings with people. The one over-arching covenant is the agreement among the members of the Godhead to provide redemption for humanity. This major covenant is worked out in history through the covenant of works (until the Fall) and the covenant of grace (from the Fall to the present). These covenants also include the Adamic covenant, the Noahic	*Description:* Dispensational theology views the world and the history of humanity as a household over which God is superintending and working out His purpose and will. In each era of history, or "dispensation", God presents humanity with a revelation of His will and a test of obedience. When humanity fails the test, God's judgment comes and a new dispensation begins. Most dispensational theologians list seven dispensations: Innocence or Freedom (Edenic), Conscience (Ante-Deluvian), Human or Civil Government (Post-Deluvian), Promise (Patriarchal),	*Description:* Some theologians have tried to chart a middle course between covenantal and dispensational theology. These recognize the basic unity of Scripture as it presents God's "Promise" or program of redemption in Jesus Christ. They also seek to account for God's relating to humanity both through what He has accomplished in the different eras of human history (dispensations) and also through what he has said at various times an in various ways (covenants).

covenant, the Abrahamic covenant, the Mosaic covenant, the Davidic covenant, and the New Covenant. Covenant theology does not see each covenant as distinct, but rather as continuously progressing toward culmination in the New Covenant.	Law (Mosaic), Grace (Present), and Kingdom (Millennium).	
Proponents: John Calvin, Johannes Cocceius, Charles Hodge, B.B. Warfield, Louis Berkhof, Marten Woudstra, Bruce Waltke	**Proponents:** J.N. Darby, C.I. Scofield, Lewis Sperry Chafer, Charles Ryrie, John Walvoord.	**Proponents:** Walter Kaiser, Henry Virkler, Scott Hafemann, some progressive dispensationalists.
Hermeneutics: Covenant theology emphasizes continuity between the Old and New Testaments, rather than discontinuity. The historical-grammatical method is primary, but prophecy is often understood as symbolically pointing to a spiritual fulfillment of the Old Testament promises of the kingdom to Israel.	**Hermeneutics:** Dispensational theology emphasizes the basic discontinuity between the Old and New Testaments. The "literal" interpretation of Scripture is central to dispensational theology. Old Testament promises of God's kingdom to Israel are to be fulfilled literally and physically.	**Hermeneutics:** Those who hold a mediating view recognize both continuity and discontinuity between the testaments. They attempt to use a consistent exegetical approach to Scripture, looking for the author's intended meaning in each passage, whether Old Testament or New Testament prophecy.

God's People: In the view of covenant theology, God has one people—the saints of the Old Testament era and the saints of the New Testament era. The Church is present in both testaments.	**God's People:** Dispensational theology teaches that God has two people— Israel and the Church. Israel is God's earthly people and the Church is God's heavenly people.	**God's People:** God has one people, with distinguishable aspects. The Church has not replaced Israel, but has been "grafted in" to the olive tree of the people of God, which has grown from its roots, the Patriarchs of Israel, and will include the "natural branches" again.
God's Plan for His People: God has one people and one plan for His people in every age since the Fall: to call out his people, the Church of both the Old and New Testament eras into one body, graciously redeeming his people through Christ.	**God's Plan for His People:** God has two distinct plans: an earthly plan for his earthly people Israel, and a heavenly plan for His heavenly people the church. God has planned an earthly kingdom for Israel, which has been postponed since He was rejected at His first coming. During the Church Age, which began at Pentecost, God is calling out a heavenly people. Dispensationalists disagree over whether Israel and the Church will remain distinct in the eternal state.	**God's Plan for His People:** God has one plan, with distinguishable aspects. God will fulfill all of His promises to Israel, and the Church— composed of redeemed people from every tribe, tongue, and nation— will enjoy the everlasting presence of God forever, as He fills the earth with His glory.
Christ's First Coming: At His first coming, Christ came to establish his spiritual and invisible kingdom through the	**Christ's First Coming:** Some dispensationalists believe that, at His first coming, Christ offered the earthly kingdom to Israel. It	**Christ's First Coming:** It was God's all-wise plan that Jesus Christ would be rejected at His first coming, so that He might become the

Church. Some covenant theologians (especially postmillennialists) believe that there is a physical aspect to Christ's present kingdom.	would have been established immediately if they had accepted Him. Other dispensationalists believe that He did inaugurate the Messianic kingdom in which the church participates, but the earthly kingdom will not be established until His Second Coming; He always intended the cross before the crown.	sacrifice for sin and accomplish redemption for the whole world. Although His physical kingdom has not yet been established, the kingdom of heaven has been inaugurated in the Church.
The New Covenant: The promises of the New Covenant mentioned in Jer. 31:31ff are fulfilled in the New Testament Church.	*The New Covenant:* Some dispensationalists believe that the New Covenant is only for Israel, while others believe that both Israel and the Church will participate in it, in distinct ways.	*The New Covenant:* The promises of the New Covenant begin to be fulfilled in any of the remnant of Israel who trust in Jesus as the Messiah, and these blessings are shared by Gentile believers as well. Jesus Christ inaugurated the New Covenant, which will reach its complete fulfillment after His Second Coming.
Eschatology: Historically, covenant theology has been either amillennial, believing that Christ's kingdom is present and spiritual, or postmillennial, believing that the Church is bringing	*Eschatology:* All dispensationalists are premillennialists; most, though not all, are pretribulationists. Dispensational premillennialists believe that in the last days God will turn the focus of His work toward Israel once again, apart from His	*Eschatology:* Among those who hold a mediating view, most are premillennial. Some believe that the Rapture will occur before Christ's Second Coming, while others (historic premillennialists) believe that the

in the kingdom now, and Christ will return after this kingdom has been established. Christ's Second Coming will be to bring final judgment and the eternal state.	work in the Church age. Christ will reign for 1000 years on David's throne in fulfillment of the Old Testament promises. According to most dispensationalists, the Rapture will occur first, then the tribulation, followed by the Second Coming and the 1000-year reign of Christ on earth. After this will come the final judgment and the eternal state.	Rapture and Christ's return will occur together after the tribulation.
Recent Developments: In recent years, some covenant theologians have begun to recognize some areas of discontinuity between the Old and New Testaments, and some contrasts between the way that saints of the Old Testament related to God and the worship experience of the saints of the New Testament era.	*Recent Developments:* In the past quarter-century, dispensationalists have made an effort to continually evaluate their stance and adjust their views according to Scripture. Recently, progressive dispensationalists have begun to recognize more continuity between the Old and New Testaments, especially regarding God's plan of salvation and the things that Israel and the church have in common.	*Recent Developments:* As the reader will see from the summaries above, there is considerable variation among those who do not classify themselves as either covenantal or dispensational. The summaries above are, admittedly, somewhat vague and nonspecific. This is intended to leave room for the variations between the particular views of those who hold to neither covenant theology nor dispensationalism.

BIBLIOGRAPHY

Baxter, J. Sidlow. *Explore the Book*. Grand Rapids: Zondervan, 1980.

Belcher, Richard P. *A Comparison of Covenant and Dispensational Theology*. Fort Mill: Richbarry Press, 1986.

Bernard, Thomas Dehany. *The Progress of Doctrine in the New Testament*. Oxford: Gordon College Press, 1864.

Edwards, Jonathan. *The History of Redemption*. Grand Rapids: Associated Publishers and Authors, 1774.

Geisler, Norman. *A Popular Survey of the Old Testament*. Grand Rapids: Baker Books, 2007.

_____. *A Popular Survey of the New Testament*. Grand Rapids: Baker Books, 2008.

Hatch, James. "The Beloved." Columbia Bible College, Columbia, S.C. Class Notes, 1972.

Hodgkin, A.M. *Christ in All the Scriptures*. London: Alfred Holness, 1909.

House, H. Wayne. *Charts of Christian Theology and Doctrine*. Grand Rapids: Zondervan, 1992.

Kaiser, Walter C. *Toward an Old Testament Theology*. Grand Rapids: Zondervan, 1991.

_____. *The Promise-Plan of God: A Biblical Theology of the Old and New Testaments*. Grand Rapids: Zondervan, 2008.

Lasor, William Sanford. *Israel*. Grand Rapids: Eerdmans, 1976.

McGrath, Alister. *Beyond the Quiet Time*. Vancouver: Regent College Publishing, 2003.

Morris, Leon. *The Apostolic Preaching of the Cross*. 3rd rev. ed. Grand Rapids: Eerdmans, 2001.

Pentecost, J. Dwight. *The Words and Works of Jesus Christ*. Grand Rapids: Zondervan, 1981.

Phillips, John. *Exploring the Scriptures*. Chicago: Moody Press, 1970.

Ryken, Leland, James C. Wilhoit, and Tremper Longman III, eds. *Dictionary of Biblical Imagery*. Downer's Grove: InterVarsity Press, 1998.

Sauer, Erich. *The Dawn of World Redemption*. London: The Paternoster Press, 1956.

_____. *The Triumph of the Crucified*. Grand Rapids: Eerdmans, 1951.

Scroggie, W. Graham. *Know Your Bible*. London: Pickering and Inglis, Ltd., 1967.

_____. *The Unfolding Drama of Redemption*. Grand Rapids: Zondervan Publishing House, 1953.

Virkler, Henry A. and Karelynne Gerber Ayayo. *Hermeneutics: Principles and Processes of Biblical Interpretation*. 2nd ed. Grand Rapids: Baker Academic, 2007.

Wegner, Paul D. *The Journey from Texts to Translations*. Grand Rapids: Baker Academic, 1999.

Wright, N.T. *The Climax of the Covenant*. Minneapolis: Fortress Press, 1993.